Public Work, Public Workers

Ralph J. Flynn

Public Work, Public Workers

Introduction by Arnold Weber
Foreword by Jerry Wurf

THE NEW REPUBLIC BOOK COMPANY, INC.

WASHINGTON, D.C.

331.89041
F 648

Published in the United States of America in 1975
by The New Republic Book Company, Inc.
1826 Jefferson Place, N.W., Washington, D.C.

Library of Congress Cataloging in Publication Data

Flynn, Ralph J
   Public work, public workers.

   Includes bibliographical references and index.
   1. Collective bargaining—Government employees—
United States. I. Title.
HD8008.F56 1975   331.89'041'350000973 75-1130
ISBN 0-915220-01-6
ISBN 0-915220-03-2 pbk.

Printed in the United States of America

DESIGNED BY BURKEY BELSER

To my wife, Margaret Breslin Flynn, and to my children: Megan, Margaret, Moira, and Ralph

Foreword

When Ralph Flynn began writing this book, he was Executive Director of the Coalition of American Public Employees. Today he remains in the thick of the struggle for public employees' rights as an official of the California Teachers Association.

I got to know Ralph three years ago, when our union joined the NEA, the International Association of Fire Fighters, and the National Treasury Employees Union in creating the Coalition of American Public Employees.

We founded CAPE to work on the national level for a collective bargaining act for public employees; against laws that discriminate against teachers and other government workers; for an end to prohibitions against political activity by public employees. In other words, to eliminate the second-class citizenship status afforded government employees and to provide a measure of power to these men and women over the forces affecting their lives.

But we really didn't anticipate that our embryonic organization would grow so quickly into a full-fledged national alliance representing more than 2.5 million public workers, and with affiliates throughout the country. Through Ralph's leadership, CAPE achieved a great deal in its first months.

In Wisconsin we removed a constitutional ceiling on public employee pensions. Some 20,000 retired state and local government workers received an immediate cost-of-living increase as a result of that effort.

In Iowa we persuaded the legislature to pass a public employee collective bargaining law. The law isn't exactly a model, but it represents a beginning.

In California our union and NEA worked together to defeat

then-Governor Reagan's proposal to write into the state constitution a limit on taxes and spending. This measure, a last gasp of Reaganism, would have had a devastating impact on schools and other public services.

But public employees won't be first-class citizens until Congress passes a Wagner Act for public employees, guaranteeing every teacher, every nurse, every clerk the right to join a union, to bargain for decent wages and proper working conditions, and to do so free from fear and recrimination.

To this battle, Ralph Flynn brings his own philosophy, one typical of the new generation of public employee unionists. He was influenced by the Catholic Worker movement, one of the best schools for social decency, and learned the nobility of public service from the noble Dorothy Day. He came into the teaching system in Boston during a period of hard times that some of us have forgotten—the years after the Korean war. When he passed the qualifying test, it was as difficult as a bar exam.

Ralph is valuable to our movement because he is the kind of person who can bring other people together. School teachers and sanitation men, fire fighters and social workers, people who came up during the Depression of the '30s and people whose careers are bumping about in the Nixon-Ford recession.

Ralph left the classroom in the '60s, but he remains a teacher— bringing the message of public employee organization to a growing and receptive army of men and women who work for government.

Washington, D.C   JERRY WURF
January 15, 1975   International President
                              American Federation of State, County,
                                and Municipal Employees (AFL-CIO)

Acknowledgments

This book could not have been written without the encouragement and support of the Board of Directors, past and present, of the Coalition of American Public Employees. And so I would like to thank Vincent Connery, president, National Treasury Employees Union; James Harris, president, National Education Association; Terry Herndon, executive secretary, National Education Association; William Lucy, secretary-treasurer of AFSCME; Jerry Wurf, president of AFSCME; and Helen Wise and Catharine Barrett, past presidents of the National Education Association. The opinions and conclusions contained in the book, however, are my own and do not necessarily reflect the policy of the Coalition.

A special debt of gratitude is owed to Fred Jordan, of Calvin Kytle Associates, Washington, D.C., who has spent hundreds of hours providing structural continuity and drafting the manuscript. Insofar as the book is coherent and readable, the credit belongs to him.

The opinions and conclusions in *Public Work, Public Workers* are, of course, the product of a lifetime, but certain individuals helped mold these views without necessarily agreeing with them. Among those to whom I am especially indebted are Alan West, retired acting executive secretary of NEA; Robert Chanin, general counsel of NEA; Dr. Wilfred Sheehan, retired executive secretary of the Connecticut Education Association; Daniel F. Flynn, my father, whose 35 years on the Boston waterfront shaped a belief in labor that has become a part of me; and Margaret A. Flynn, my mother, whose pragmatic Nova Scotian view of life taught me that dreams can be made workable.

Washington, D.C.   RALPH J. FLYNN
January 1975

Introduction

The public sector was long regarded as an obscure, if not well-appointed, corner of the American industrial relations scene. In contrast to his counterpart in private employment, the public employee was viewed as nested in a secure job insulated from the buffeting of the competitive market. He presumably held a white-collar job that was divorced from the pressures and day-to-day accumulation of inequities that characterized the plant floor or the assembly line. If he wasn't the highest-paid fellow in his neighborhood, at least he was the most secure, and he could look forward to the pleasures of a generous pension at retirement.

Under these circumstances, unionization and collective bargaining were alien or distasteful concepts. If a few visionaries saw collective bargaining as devices to improve the lot of the public employee, they were viewed as provocateurs or eccentrics. Since the authority of public management was buttressed by the "sovereignty doctrine" (the king can do no wrong), collective bargaining was generally considered to be irrelevant if not illegal.

In the last 15 years this idyllic picture has been dramatically confronted with reality. Since 1960 the most dynamic and turbulent developments in labor relations have taken place in the public sector. With the promulgation of Executive Order 10988, President John Kennedy extended the rights of union organization and a truncated system of collective bargaining to federal employees. This action exerted pressure at the state level and laws giving public employees the right of union organization and collective bargaining soon were enacted in major states such as New York, Michigan, and Pennsylvania.

These changes in the legal environment set the stage for a virtual explosion of unionization among public employees. By 1974 the public sector had become more highly unionized than private industry. The reverberations from this explosion are still being felt throughout the various layers of government and the political structure. The public has become accustomed to strikes of garbage collectors, teachers, drawbridge operators, welfare workers, and even policemen. In addition, the process of organization is still under way. Many states do not have laws that extend the right of organization to public employees, and the issue of the use of power through strikes is still the subject of intense controversy.

Despite the fact that the legal foundation has not been completed, the process has set in motion changes in the status of public employees and their relationships to government and the broader society that cannot be reversed. Walter Reuther, the former president of the United Automobile Workers, sought to use the UAW and the labor movement as a vehicle to change the nature of society. Ultimately, he had to be content with changing the nature of working conditions in the automobile plants. In contrast, public employee unions are striving to alter working conditions in the firehouse, the classroom, and the welfare office—and will end up changing the distribution of power in governmental structures and, hence, in society in general.

In this book Ralph Flynn provides a sharp perspective and human detail to labor relations in the public sector. He demonstrates that dealing with governmental bureaucracy can be as frustrating as working on the assembly line. He argues that civil service procedures may not provide the protection and sense of dignity that advocates of this personnel system attribute to it. And he vividly paints a picture of what happens to a community when it is beset by a strike of policemen, garbage collectors, and other public employees who provide essential services.

One does not have to agree with Flynn to appreciate the thrust of his message: that public employees are concerned with problems and grievances that are fundamentally similar to those confronted by employees in the private sector, and that the process of resolving these grievances has not been abetted by the patchwork of laws and regulations that presently exists. Flynn ultimately makes the (his) case for the enactment of a federal statute that will uniformly govern the organization of public employees at all levels of government. For many students of labor relations, this alternative may be too sweeping and, certainly, other policy options should be explored. However, few observers of labor relations will quarrel with his central premise. The great achievement of the American industrial relations system in the private sector has been the development of the rule of law and of procedures whereby conflict has been mediated and even turned to constructive uses. This achievement is yet to be registered in the public sector and the longer it takes, the higher the cost to society will be.

Pittsburgh   ARNOLD R. WEBER
January 13, 1975   Provost of Carnegie-Mellon University
University Dean,
Graduate School of Industrial Relations

Contents

Foreword by Jerry Wurf   vii

Acknowledgments   ix

Introduction by Arnold Weber   xi

 1. Some Are More Equal Than Others   1

 2. Today Is 1934   6

 3. Downpayment on Tomorrow   12

 4. For God's Sake, What Do These People Want?   22

 5. It's Impossible to Govern This City!   34

 6. Problem-Solving and the Myth of Omnipotence   47

 7. A Plague on Both Your Houses   58

 8. Tell Me How We Got Here . . .   77

 9. . . . And I'll Tell You How We Get Home   82

10. A New Kind of Management, A New Kind of Labor   99

Index   107

1. Some Are More Equal Than Others

When Congress passed the National Labor Relations Act in 1935, it made it

> the policy of the United States to eliminate the causes of certain substantial obstructions to the free flow of commerce and to mitigate and eliminate these obstructions when they have occurred by encouraging the practice and procedure of collective bargaining and by protecting the exercise by workers of full freedom of association, self-organization and designation of representatives of their own choosing, for the purpose of negotiating the terms and conditions of their employment or other mutual aid or protection.

Two phrases in that paragraph, "policy of the United States" and "collective bargaining," were crucial to the millions of union members who were trying to cope with the devastating depression that was then engulfing the United States. For the National Labor Relations Act—popularly known as the Wagner Act—was a grant of federal power to working men and women and their unions to right the imbalance of economic power between labor and capital that had helped plunge the country into that crisis in the first place.

Today, those same phrases are still the keys to the plight of 14 million American workers who are *not* protected by the Wagner Act: the employees of our federal, state, and local governments. This book is about those 14 million men and women and what is happening to them as a matter of public policy. It is about the denial of the protections of their labor that were granted to their counterparts in private industry nearly 40 years ago. R. L. Glover is one of these people.

You don't ask what the "R. L." in R. L. Glover stands for. He's from Texas and considers himself a Southerner, so Robert (E.) Lee might be a good guess. But a guess will have to do. You don't ask. Not because he's unfriendly, but because there is in his manner a sense of dignity and privacy not to be violated.

Tall, sunburned, wide-hipped, he looks like he could have been a semipro pitcher back in the days when he carried 50 fewer pounds on the kind of frame sportswriters call rawboned. He wears a masonic ring, chain-smokes Kents, and drinks as many as 15 cups of black coffee daily.

Homer Eley is his partner on occasional trips to Washington, D.C. He is just under medium height but looks shorter, sitting or standing, next to R. L. Nearing 50, Eley has dark hair that looks like the rest of him: neat, in place, just-showered. He has the look of a sailor who has a good duty station on his ship. His hands don't fidget when he talks; his eyes survey the middle distance, until he gets to the point of what he wants to say and he hits on the way he wants to say it. Then they come to rest on you, lightly, politely.

Both men are friendly in a reticent way, not gregarious tellers of tall tales about Texas where both were born, grew up, and still live, R. L. in East Dallas, Homer in nearby Garland. Characteristically, on their trips to Washington they always try to fly Braniff, out of loyalty to a union colleague whose relative works for the airline.

When they are not driving buses that weigh 16,000 pounds, are 40 feet long and "all-the-law-allows" wide for the Dallas Transit System, they preside together over a diminished labor union, Local Division 1338 of the Amalgamated Transit Union, a venerable American labor organization that goes back more than 80 years. Its motto: "Freedom through Organization." Homer is secretary-treasurer of 1338. R. L., senior in age (62) and transit service, is president. They are caretakers of a union that once took care of itself.

R. L. started out in 1938 with the old Dallas Railway and Terminal Company as a streetcar operator. He did that for nine years before switching over to bus driving in 1947, and he remembers those nine years with pleasure. "The only reason I transferred to buses was that they took all the streetcars off," he says and laughs. "That was a great life. Anybody who hasn't ever operated streetcars has missed half of their life. That was altogether different than operating a bus."

He and Eley, who operated streetcars for a shorter time after he came out of navy service in World War II, can still remember the end-of-the-line drill: Remove the reverse key and take it to the other end of the car with your fare box, reverse the passenger seats, change your trolley pole, pull the other pole down. They have forgotten about one step: Change the "white" and "colored" section signs.

R. L. feels no nostalgia, however, for the conditions that prevailed in the transit company back when he first started working there. "Conditions were so miserable that in the early forties the times just became ripe for a union," he remembers. Several attempts earlier in the thirties to organize the workers had failed. "They had to meet in back alleys and behind sign boards and at midnight," he recalls, and management fired the would-be union members. But finally, the international sent in organizers, and the first union contract was signed in 1943.

The 1940s and early 1950s were good years for public transportation and for Local 1338. Growth in population and shortages of automobiles and gasoline insured that "we had more business than we could really take care of," R. L. remembers. The number of transit passengers grew, and union membership—and strength—increased. At its peak in the late 1950s, Local 1338 had more than 1200 members, 100 percent of the drivers, mechanics, and related workers in the bargaining unit.

As production of cars, gasoline, and highways hit its stride, however, America's fabled love affair with the automobile had its effect on public transportation, in Dallas as in the rest of the country. Ridership began to fall, service was cut back, and the number of transit workers gradually declined. In 1960 control of the company passed under new management. "Then it really went down," R. L. recalls. The new owner "completely gutted the system."

In spite of these changes, the union retained the greater percentage of its eligible membership all through those years and continued to function. Its contract gave the president and vice president leaves of absence from their jobs and continued seniority with the company, so they could provide leadership full time to the men and women of 1338. The officers bargained for wage increases and negotiated on hours and working conditions. The local had a strong grievance procedure, that, after time, the company came to rely on to sort out many of its personnel problems.

Then, in 1964, the city of Dallas bought the transit system, and the bottom fell out of Local 1338. Texas Civil Statutes provide that it is against public policy for state officials or officials of the political subdivisions to enter into collective bargaining agreements with a labor organization as a bargaining agent. "They did away with our checkoff of dues and failed to recognize our union and our officers. They canceled our president's and vice president's leaves of absence and told them to report back to work or they'd be terminated," R. L. says. "Neither one of them came back, so they were terminated."

The union treasury dwindled, and its staff was let go. Eventually Glover was elected president, and Eley, secretary-treasurer. But they do union work strictly on their off hours. Both men work full time, getting up before dawn to roll their buses out on the streets according to split-second schedules.

Union work doesn't consist of much now that the men and women of 1338 are public employees, and although the jobs the union members perform haven't changed from what they did before the takeover, the conditions of their employment are far different. There is no collective bargaining, no strong grievance procedure. "Oh, we can go in every year, with our hats in our hands, to make 'requests,'" R. L. says in disgust. "And they say, 'Thank you very much, but there isn't any money in next year's budget for what you want.'"

"There's no negotiations, no job security; you don't have anything," Homer says. "The turnover rate is 10 out of 14, and most of that is terminations—new men getting fired because they have a hard time adjusting to the drastic change in working hours for a bus driver, getting up at 3:30 or four o'clock in the morning to move that bus out.

"We try to represent these men, but city officials remind us we don't have any right to go in with them," Homer says. "They are always reminding us that we have no official standing with them."

"There was a time when the company wouldn't fire a man without checking with the union first," R.L. adds. "They knew we'd be raising hell to get him back his job, unless he'd been stealing or drinking or, you know, something immoral like that."

What can the president of Local 1338 do about getting better wages for his members? "Nothing but make requests," says R. L. "It's not a good living, now. Most bus drivers' wives work. If it weren't for the spouses' working, it would be awful hard to make out. Now down in Houston, they still have collective bargaining. Their rates are way above ours." Retirement benefits too have shrunk in the face of inflation. "And we can't do anything about it," R. L. says.

It is the loss of standing the union had as the bargaining representative of its members that troubles R. L. and Homer most. Where the members of 1338 once could strike if they didn't like the terms offered, they cannot now. Where the local once had a say in decisions affecting the livelihood of its members, it has none now.

With one exception. Federal law requires that when the transit system applies for federal demonstration grants, the city's application must be accompanied by an agreement with the local that protects the jobs of existing transit workers. Without the approval of 1338, the city's funding request doesn't stand a chance. So every so often, R. L., Homer, and 1338 become real in the city's eyes. The city of Dallas asks them to go to Washington to assure the federal government that 1338 blesses the application for funds. And the two men borrow this federal power to negotiate for what they can get for 1338.

For a moment, 1338 is once again a bargaining unit. Then it's all over for another spell. R. L. and Homer get on a plane and fly home to Dallas. The next morning, they are up in time to get rush-hour passengers to their jobs.

Why did things change so radically for Local 1338 from one day to the next in 1964? Why did a healthy union cease to be? Why did membership dwindle till it now includes only 540 members? How did "Freedom through Organization" become just a slogan?

"They didn't say but one thing to us when the city took over: Public unions are against the law," R. L. answers. "And they are."

2. Today Is 1934

The contrast between Local 1338 of the Amalgamated Transit Union when its workers were part of private industry and the union's role today dramatically emphasizes just what the passage of the Wagner Act has meant to many American workers. But the legal rights to organize and bargain collectively did not just fall off a tree. They were developed out of the widespread suffering the Depression visited on working Americans and out of a new determination by unions and union members to have something to say about "the terms and conditions of their employment." That determination reached its fiercest point in 1934.

Labor historian Irving Bernstein has written in *The Turbulent Years:*

> A handful of years bears a special quality in American labor history. There occurred at these times strikes and social upheavals of extraordinary importance, drama and violence which ripped the cloak of civilized decorum from society, leaving exposed naked class conflict. Such a year was 1886, with the great strikes of the Knights of Labor and the Haymarket Riot. Another was 1894, with the shattering conflict of Eugene Debs's American Railway Union against the Pullman Company and the government of the United States. Nineteen thirty-four must be added to this roster.

The decade of the 1920s was a nightmare for American labor: Declining membership, dwindling influence, harassment by the courts, conservative national leadership, and, finally, the economic collapse of 1929 brought most American unions to their knees. Many were bankrupt and could not even hold their annual conventions. The mightiest of them all, the United Mine Workers, disintegrated. Unemployment grew exponentially each year from 1929 to 1932—

500,000, 4 million, 5 million, 6 million, 9 million. Wages plummeted. When Franklin Roosevelt took office in March of 1933, there were 15 million unemployed workers and many more on short hours. Bread lines and soup kitchens gave way to widespread scavenging for food in restaurant garbage cans and at the city dump.

But that year, for the first time in a long while, labor once again was welcome at the White House. Its leaders' views were sought, listened to, and acted upon. Section 7(a) of the National Industrial Recovery Act of 1933 granted workers the right to organize themselves and elect representatives of their own choosing to bargain collectively with management over wages, hours, and working conditions. As a result union organizing drives met with instant success. "The people have been so starved out that they are flocking to the Union by the thousands," organizer Garfield Lewis wrote to United Mine Workers Vice President Philip Murray from the coal fields of traditionally anti-union Kentucky. "I organized nine locals Tuesday." New blood was flowing into the moribund body of organized labor.

If 1933 seemed like a dream year, 1934 was the year of awakening. Drafting NIRA was the work of many hands with not much time to pause over details. Along with its guarantees to labor, Section 7(a) conceded to employers that where existing employee organizations were satisfactorily representing employees, they could be recognized. That opened the way to company unions. Just as serious, the act established no congressionally sanctioned way of enforcing the section, opening a loophole that Roosevelt sought to plug by creating, by executive order, a National Labor Board.

It was becoming clear that most employers had no intention of complying with Section 7(a). As newly organized unions confronted management with demands, they were met by blunt refusals to bargain. Strikes were called. The Labor Board responded gallantly and was developing "a common law" applying to the resolution of such confrontations, when it was challenged for lack of statutory authority by Weirton Steel and Budd Manufacturing. The board was brought to its knees. The final blow came from the President himself. Fearful that a looming strike in the fledgling auto industry would jeopardize national economic recovery, Roosevelt exempted that industry from the requirements of Section 7(a). The message was clear: Employers would not obey the law, and the government could not make them.

Bitterly awakened from the dream of 1933, the unions determined to rely only on their own strength — the strike — to combat the employers' strength — the dollar — and to establish for themselves the right to collective bargaining.

In the spring and summer of 1934 a wave of strikes washed across the country. In Toledo the unemployed — normally the pool from which management recruited strikebreakers — supported a new union of Auto-Lite workers and stayed with them through tear gas, bullets, and an assault by the National Guard until the company agreed to collective bargaining. Two persons died.

In Minneapolis truckers used brilliant planning and organizing to make good on their promise that "not a wheel will roll" until the union was recognized and bargaining begun. Through 36 days of violence on a grand scale, they made it stick and won recognition and wage increases. Five persons died.

On the West Coast, longshoremen closed down every major port and in San Francisco sparked one of the few general strikes in the nation's history before a bitterly anti-union business establishment agreed to terms that ended the loathsome "shape-up" method of hiring dock labor. Two persons were killed.

The 1934 strikes surprised employers with their ferocity, their strength, and their outcomes. Management had hoped that an unsuccessful strike would permanently break unionism in their towns; 1934 was their year to be bitterly disappointed. Even so, as a group, they continued their opposition to labor unions and to 7(a).

The strikes educated many in the federal government, if not the President himself. It confirmed that new legislation beyond the National Industrial Recovery Act was needed to deal with strikes and to encourage economic recovery.

One who was not surprised and who needed little education was Senator Robert F. Wagner, Sr., of New York, the New Deal's outstanding labor expert. "By the end of 1933," Irving Bernstein wrote, "Wagner had become convinced that the National Labor Board's 'common law' should be incorporated into a permanent statute, that the administrative agency should be outside the National Recovery Administration structure, and the enforcement powers should be provided to deal with noncompliance such as was faced in the Weirton and Budd cases."

Wagner introduced his legislation March 1, 1934, too close to adjournment to get congressional approval in the face of Roosevelt's ambivalence toward the measure. But it was not too late to draw a hail of fire from the National Association of Manufacturers, employers, company unions, and the Communists. At first amended nearly to death, then shunted aside in favor of a resolution loosely arming the President with powers to confront a pending strike in the steel industry, the bill was not acted on. Roosevelt still wanted to be free to deal with recovery without the constraints a labor law might have placed upon him.

Wagner paid close attention to his opposition's cries that the bill was unconstitutional. In redrafting it that fall and winter, he took care to immunize the bill from the Supreme Court's recent and withering wrath at a string of social legislation.

The bill was reintroduced in February of 1935. Again, the National Association of Manufacturers mounted a strong campaign against it with the support of newspapers on both the left and the right. The American Federation of Labor vigorously lobbied for the bill, and an early and unexpected test vote in the Senate led to prompt approval in that body.

Then, the Supreme Court issued its decision invalidating important provisions of the Recovery Act, including Section 7(a), and clouding the bill's possible constitutionality. But the memories of the violence of the preceding spring and summer outweighed fears of what might or might not happen. Despite the Supreme Court threat, President Roosevelt changed his position. He adopted the bill as his own, supported Senator Wagner's generalship of it, and after its passage by the House of Representatives, signed it on July 5, 1935.

To me, even the most telescoped retelling, like this one, of the story of the fight for collective bargaining emits strong whiffs of the excitement, the danger, the dedication, and the desperation of those times, though I was too young to know anything of these events when they happened. Yet the story only seems to bore many younger men and women. They sing the old songs of the period, it is true. But often they do not know they are singing union songs, let alone that the song "Which Side Are You On?" which served the antiwar protest so often, was written by a woman of the coal country — Florence Reece — just hours after a strikebreaking deputy sheriff ransacked her home and terrorized her family searching for her union-organizer husband. Would they be interested to know that the hymn of the civil rights movement, "We Shall Overcome," was first a union organizing song called "We Will Overcome"? Maybe not.

Some older people who lived through those times are saddened that this is so. They feel that members of today's generation are turning their backs on an important part of our social heritage. They are not interested in a struggle 40 years ago that deserves their attention if for no other reason than because it did so much to make possible the good life they enjoy.

It is the irony in this situation that is striking. Today's seeming indifference to labor's "war stories" of the 1930s is just another measure of the success of collective bargaining in the private sector. For the Wagner Act did more than institutionalize, in the new National Labor Relations Board, the "common law" developed by the Old National Labor Board. It did more, too, than extend Section 7(a) and provide for its full enforcement. It made it the policy of this land that there should be equity between the employer and his employee. The worker's right to protect his labor was raised up equal with the manager's right to protect his investors' money. It established principles on which labor and management, over the next 40 years, built relatively cooperative and reasonably fair relations, cooperative and fair enough to help make this the most productive economy in the world.

Cardinal among those principles is that collective bargaining is the employee's right. Relying on it, labor and management have bargained out enviable wages, hours, working conditions, and profitability. And they have mended Professor Bernstein's "ripped cloak of civilized decorum" to once again clothe the "naked class conflict" of the 1930s. Resolving disputes unresolvable through collective bargaining has become a respected profession for which young men and women prepare in schools of industrial and labor relations around the country.

The emergence of collective bargaining as public policy has created comparative stability for both sides in the private sector, and, as a concomitant, the former militancy of unions has faded. Equity, rights, stability are easy to get used to when one has them. But 14 million Americans, whose rights as workers are not insured by a Wagner Act, don't have them. And for them these rights are still worth fighting for. Public sector employees are governed by a patchwork of state laws that range from reasonable on the sparse end of the scale to punitive on the other, where too many states, like Texas, stand. For the most part, these workers have only limited rights to bargain with their employers about the "terms and conditions of their employment," and nowhere do they have the rights granted to their private sector counterparts by the Wagner Act. In no case is the public worker's right to protect his labor equal to his employer's right to direct that labor. And in only a handful of cases have equitable principles been established upon which public labor and public management can build the fair and cooperative relationships necessary to do the public business and do it in reasonable harmony.

In some ways today is 1934 in the public sector. Public employees are joining unions in unprecedented numbers. Though they don't have the right to strike (except in limited form in Hawaii and Pennsylvania), they have the power. The incidence of public sector strikes is growing geometrically. These strikes, increasingly, are bitter and long. The cloak of civilized decorum is, once again, ripping.

The country, the Congress, and public employers and employees have two options in meeting a situation that is becoming more and more dangerous. We can learn from the history of the Wagner Act and guarantee collective bargaining to public employees as national policy. That is the road to stability and partnership in public labor relations. Or we can ignore history and, in the process, rediscover it painfully and expensively. That is the road to more and more garbage strikes, such as the one in Memphis in 1968, to transit strikes, like the one in San Francisco in 1974, and mass walkouts of public school teachers.

3. Downpayment
on Tomorrow

In 1970 the 73.5 million workers in the civilian labor force of this country were arrayed as follows across the Bureau of Labor Statistics' nine categories of employment:

manufacturing	19 million
trade	15 million
government	13 million
services	12 million
transportation and public utilities	0.4 million
finance, insurance, and real estate	3.5 million
agriculture	3 million
contract construction	3 million
mining	1 million

Most of the nation's workers, manifestly, are in industries producing services as opposed to those producing goods. The production of goods—raising food crops, building, extracting minerals, and manufacturing goods—has required less than half of the country's work force since the late 1940s. In that era the number of employees in these jobs reached about 25 million, where it has more or less stayed since then. The hallmark of the goods-producing sector of the economy in this time span has been increasing productivity per worker, thanks mainly to the advent of automation.

In roughly the same time span the number of workers in all the service-producing industries has grown from about 25 million in 1947 to 47.3 million in 1970. From 1960 to 1970 alone, the growth in the number of service-industry workers amounted to 13.5 million.

The major factors underlying this rapid jump since the end of World War II are the nation's growing population, that population's marked tendency to congregate in metropolitan areas, the concomitant growth in demand for the kinds of services that are needed to support life at urban densities, and Americans' rising income and living standards, which create the demand and pay the bill for improved services. These, then, are the ingredients of what has come to be known as the postindustrial society that is the United States.

But to appreciate the magnitude of the postindustrial changes in both the goods- and services-producing aspects of our economy, the memories of a man approaching 40 can be far more telling than statistics. I think, for instance, of the things that were not in general supply until I was nearly 25 years old: television sets (black and white only), refrigerators with large freezer compartments in them, dishwashers, nuclear power generators, power-assisted windows on cars, blinking turn signals, Teflon-coated skillets, gas-powered lawn mowers, pop-up tents and other lightweight camping gear, plastic shoes. If I go back 25 years, to when I was 15, the list includes automatic transmissions on automobiles, small foreign cars, electric ranges, deep freezes (there were freezer lockers at the local freezer plant instead), smog, contact lenses, freeways, stereo record players.

Just as one can objectify the transformation in the goods-producing sector of our economy over the past quarter century by inventorying his memory of physical goods, so, too, can one point to the changes on its services-producing side, especially where services are provided through the public purse. This task is more difficult, because services are rarely tangible, and public services, for reasons that dwell deep in the American psyche, are less valued and, therefore, less memorable than non-publicly provided services.

In trying to visualize the growth in demand for these public services, one has to recognize the two dimensions that are involved. First, there is the growth of demand for services in all the traditional service categories—health, education, recreation—occasioned by a growing and increasingly metropolitan national population. Where there were 151,326,000 people in the United States in 1950, there are today 213,212,000. And where, near the beginning of the post-World War II era (1950) 54,479,000 of us lived in rural areas and 96,847,000 lived in urban areas, today 75 percent of us are massed in the nation's sprawling, nearly continuous metropolitan areas.

Second, one must consider the growth in demand for new kinds of services within the traditional service categories. Twenty-five years ago, the family without sufficient resources to send a mentally ill member to a private "sanitorium"—which is to say, the average American family—had but one alternative for treatment: the state mental hospital. Today, there are alternatives in the community. The quality of these may not be all we would like it to be, but certainly, in almost all cases, these programs are better and more effective than the "snake pit" state hospitals of the thirties, forties, and fifties.

In the field of education the growth of services in response to demand has been staggering. Back then school was school. Period. There was one curriculum, one method of administration, and one faculty, whose preparation varied only by virtue of the field of knowledge in which an individual had chosen to teach. Today, school is a series of programs: programs for the bright, programs for the dull, programs for the handicapped. An essentially academic curriculum has given way to one that is heavily, if not predominantly, vocational.

And the range of choices beyond high school has widened with the growth of these educational services. Where previously one either went to college or to work after high school, there is now a third alternative—junior or community college—and perhaps a fourth— work *cum* junior college.

This expansion of educational alternatives is being overlapped by a genuine revolution in our concept of education and its purposes for the individual and the society. The revolution goes under the label "life curriculum," and it is causing the breakup of the old, static notion of education as something that takes place between kindergarten and grade 12 for most people, in college years 1 through 4 for a select few, and in graduate schools for an even smaller number.

The "k-12" system, manifestly, still exists. But it is rapidly becoming to education what the veriform appendix is to the human body—a vestigial remain. The new essence of American education is the concept of education as a process that begins with birth and continues to death.

The life curriculum revolution has been made possible by three developments, each one in itself seminal: First, the considerable expansion in our understanding of the ways in which very small children learn has effected enormous potential for change in early childhood education. Second, there has been great growth in the attention paid to adult education, both in the courses that are offered to those out of school and in the educational facilities available to them. Third, the development of the community college within the education hierarchy has been dramatic, going far beyond expansion of the educational alternatives available to school-age and "adult" students and affecting the nature of both curriculum and instruction.

These changes in the traditional k-12 educational system are directly affected by the controversy that has raged around the supply of teachers for public classrooms. During the halcyon years of the 1950s and 1960s, there was a vast expansion in both the education plant and in the number of teachers. By contrast, in the fall of 1973, 307,000 graduate teachers were scrambling for 117,000 jobs, according to *Teacher Supply and Demand in Public Schools*, published by the research department of the National Education Association.

In those two decades, the nation observed, or was party to, or guilty of, some of the most uncontrolled growth that any social institution has experienced. I can remember listening to Dr. Arthur Corey, executive secretary emeritus of the California Teachers Association, pleading with the State Assembly in California not to lower its credential requirements, as each year Los Angeles would come in pleading that another 3,000 teacher bodies were needed in their classrooms. The State Board of Certification would engage in ritual discussion, lower the requirements, and Los Angeles would get its bodies. Whenever some brave soul brought up the question of what was going to happen when the population line leveled out, the response was: "Well, then we can begin addressing ourselves to the issue of class size."

Well, now the babies are gone, and we've been presented with a magnificent opportunity to confront the class-size issue and do something about it. But this opportunity has been lost in the shuffle, and the problem now is popularly regarded as one of an oversupply of teachers. The class-size statistics that were perceived as an emergency situation in the 1960s are looked upon today as a reasonable norm in computing teacher supply and demand. Using the National Education Association's quality criterion, the demand for new teachers in 1973 should have been 826,000 positions rather than the 117,000 actually available. That represents a deficit of more than 400,000 graduates.

In the short term, teachers will undoubtedly use their energies in a battle for survival rather than in ways more productive for them, their students, and education as a whole. But this battle should not last overlong, because of the life curriculum concept. That will, I think, create a demand for educational programs that do not exist and a system for delivering education in ways and at hours and in places for which, at present, there is no system. By 1980 the statistics on which the "oversupply of teachers" argument is being based will have become essentially meaningless.

As for other changes in the services-producing side of our economy, they are evident all around us. There always have been parks to go to, but what is in the parks has multiplied considerably: bicycle paths, tennis and shuffleboard courts, imaginative play areas for children, even supervised recreation. And beyond the neighborhood, there is the growth in the number of campgrounds in natural areas previously inaccessible to all but the richest or the hardiest.

The last few years have seen the development of Medicare, Medicaid, Judicare, and Judicaid. There are senior citizen centers and child day care centers. There are environmental monitoring stations that alert us to dangerous concentrations of pollution in the air we breathe. There is water quality control testing and reclamation. There are centers for recycling our trash. Where we used to blister the pavement in front of our houses burning the leaves of autumn, the county now collects them for us and our grass cuttings as well.

In each of these cases a new or expanded service almost always means a need for people to offer it—people who must be located, recruited, and trained. Often they must have special education, which, in turn, puts a further demand on schools and colleges.

All these demands—whether for new or for traditional services—have made public sector employment the growth area in the U.S. labor force. Though the category of trade is the largest subgroup within the service-producing element of the American economy (almost 15 million in 1970), government employment has grown faster than any other industry division regardless of sector. In 1947 the combined employment of state, local, and federal governments was 5 million. Just between 1960 and 1970 it increased by more than 50 percent to almost 13 million. Most recent estimates put it at 14 million. By 1980, according to the Bureau of Labor Statistics, government employment may be as much as 33 percent higher than in 1970 or 16,758,000. By comparison, the trade employment group is expected by the bureau to grow at a slower 18 percent to the end of the decade, for a 1980 projected total of 17,582,000.

As it did in the 1960s, growth in public employment will take place mostly at the state and local government levels. By 1980 the bureau estimates state and local governments could be employing as many as 13.8 million workers, about 40 percent higher than in 1970. Federal government employment is expected to rise slowly to about 3 million in 1980, 11 percent more than its 1970 level of 2.7 million.

It is worth pointing out that the bureau's projections do not take into account the Product X factor, the unforeseen invention or development that always throws off the economists' projections of future economic growth or decline. The transistor tube, the cheap contraceptive pill, and the Arab capture of the world's oil-pricing mechanism are examples.

In the field of public services, life curriculum is an immediate illustration of a Product X, but there are others—some of them with a retarding effect on the demand for services in a certain area.

If, for example, Congress were to pass a minimum family income program as a solution to the oft-invoked welfare mess, whether it were like the family assistance program of the Nixon administration or some other, there might be a considerable depression in the market for social workers. If, on the other hand, the pressure to reform what is euphemistically called our penal system reaches great proportions, it is conceivable that a whole new service (and employment) area of life adjustment might be developed. This would involve psychiatric rehabilitation, advances in the care and treatment of sociopaths, and others kinds of activities that would make the demand for trained social workers and for higher quality social skills heavy indeed.

If the country gets serious about the rate at which the natural environment is being degraded, and Congress passes an action program to deal with the degradation, there might develop still another new set of services, and with them jobs that now don't even have names. All told, the bureau's projections for 1980 will probably turn out to be conservative.

Taken on balance, the growth of public employment, both recorded and projected, represents an economic and manpower phenomenon the likes of which, short of wartime, this country has not seen. But these changes represent something else, too: a commitment to improving the quality of American life that has benefited all of us. The expansion of services through public auspices that these figures represent has made the American dream more attainable by millions of people. It marks us as a more humane nation than we once were, a nation that still has not learned how to stop producing the human wastage that so many public workers are committed by their work to salvage, but one that has at least owned up to its responsibility toward those it has, in one way or another, damaged.

Our society, through the services it provides, still has not learned to arrange its affairs so that the streets of our cities are safe and pleasant. But it has found a place in its schools for thousands and thousands of educable mentally retarded children so that they can find a place later for themselves in the society outside the classroom. We have not learned fully to respect either man or nature. But we have offered a measure of security to older citizens against the economic and physical ravages of illness. We do not treat one another with equity. But we have given access to our legal system and its protections to hundreds of thousands who have not known these things before.

What we have done through the expansion of public services— inadequate as it is and inherently flawed as many of them are—is to make a down payment on a better country. This is what, in essence, the figures telling the growth of public sector employment mean. And the projections of future growth represent a commitment to further investments in the same purpose.

That this investment could also represent a decade of witless and unnecessary labor strife in the public sector is a matter of intense concern to me and a source of rising disgust. For if we do not find a better, more sensible way of regulating public sector labor relations, what lies ahead may be another 1934, a series of intensely bitter and violent strikes.

The investment is not just one of hope; it is also one of dollars. In fiscal 1973, the year for which the latest figures are available, Americans invested $121.2 billion in paying public workers on the state, federal, and local government levels to provide these services. (These figures do not include the military.) Of that, $35.2 billion was gross salary payroll to federal employees, and $86 billion was to state and local employees. Using the Bureau of Labor Statistics estimate of continued growth to 1980, one can figure roughly that the federal investment could be $39 billion by that date; the state and local outlay around $120 billion, using fiscal year 1973 pay rates.

How it is that such a sizable investment of both money and hope can be exposed to the vagaries of labor-management relations as they exist at present in America's public sector? How did we get into this mess?

The answer has two parts. First we followed a combination of both our best and our worst instincts or social attitudes. Second, as will become clearer in Chapter 8, we repeatedly failed to understand the strengths and weaknesses of our federal system and to lodge responsibilities accordingly to the governments within that system.

Here, let's talk about attitudes. According to one set of attitudes public employment is a job for weaklings, for those underendowed with both intellect and ambition. "Those who can, do; those who can't, teach," said Bernard Shaw, and his witty epigram characterizes an American attitude toward its public servants that has been as real as it is unjust.

That attitude is alloyed with another, one of envy for the stability and security of public employment. This attitude becomes particularly keen during times of economic unrest. It stems from a time when public employment was, in fact, the most secure kind of work a person could do, even though it was poorly paid. That it has become less stable is a reality that has done very little to disturb the myth of the public job as a cushy berth.

Third, there is a pronounced American preference for the things that serve one's personal ease over those things that serve the community beyond one's driveway. This has been characterized by the phrase "private opulence and public squalor." It is an attitude that John Kenneth Galbraith identified and brilliantly illuminated in *The Affluent Society.*

From this amalgam of social orientations comes, if not an active desire, at least a broad tolerance for treating public workers, economically and in other ways, as second-class citizens. They are said to be "supping at the public trough" and have been called "tax eaters, not taxpayers." There is the quaint theory that divides the world of work between constructive (private) and parasitic (public) endeavor. All these speak of America's derogation of its public workers.

The reform instinct, too, has played its part in creating the disorder of public sector labor relations in America. If one half of our attitudes has debased public work, the other has exalted it beyond reason. Episodes of municipal reform have alternated with periods of municipal corruption in U.S. history. Those episodes, prompted as they were by repeated offenses, seem to have sustained an enduring, if generalized, movement toward good government still in evidence today.

Certainly the offenses were real, and reforms were needed. But the instruments of reform, probably because they were so difficult to forge in the fire of municipal politics, have taken on the status of holy relics. Adequate to their times, they now bind us to old myths, when present realities demand new efforts. Among these relics are civil service systems, independent and autonomous school boards, the "science" of public administration, state control of municipal taxing power, fragmentation of mayoral authority, and the concept of nondelegable sovereignty.

From the good government movement there is an attitudinal

legacy as well. Born, no doubt, in the overkill of reformist zeal to demonstrate the importance of putting political and governmental function in the "right hands," one prevalent attitude is exaltation of the public business—hence, the term "public servant" and the insistence that the public employee, like Caesar's wife, be above reproach. Attitudes, of course, change. But it takes years for them to disappear entirely, and this attitude of exaltation is no exception. A strict but imprecise code of personal and group conduct still applies to public workers. There remain schools in this country where it is considered a breach of this code for a teacher, particularly a woman, to be seen by students or parents smoking a cigarette.

One of the injunctions transmitted by this code can be summed up in the old saying, "Be good, dear child; let who will be clever." For the good public servant, organizing for the purposes of collective bargaining was too clever by half. The public business, the line went, was far too noble to be subjected by its servants to the democratic processes of collective bargaining. This attitude was widespread enough that public employee organization leaders themselves were loath to associate their groups too closely with that practice or concept. Even today a number of teachers who are members of the National Education Association prefer to describe what the association does in their behalf as something other than collective bargaining.

Finally, there is the American attitude toward services as opposed to goods. The difference between the two has never really been understood. We keep trying to define services in terms of goods, or, more accurately, to set the worth of services in relation to the worth of goods. I remember once listening to Sargent Shriver attempting to explain to a group of intelligent, able businessmen why the percentage of his Office of Economic Opportunity budget going to salaries was so much greater than the percentage of their own budgets dedicated to wages. Shriver was a talented explicator, a gifted evangel, of the program he headed. Again and again he explained that OEO's product was services to poor people, not the production of widgets or airplanes. It takes people to give services to people. That's what services are, he explained: people doing something for other people. OEO didn't buy much in the way of raw materials and had nothing in the way of manufacturing costs, he said. A greater percentage of his budget went to salaries, because, after rent, typewriter ribbons, and paper, that's really all there was to spend it on. Again and again, his audience didn't get it. To them, such a high percentage of budget devoted to salaries only confirmed their

worst fears of bureaucratic featherbedding. Mayor Henry Maier of
Milwaukee has said that it now costs $37 to get 100 dead cats off the
streets of his city. It may seem outrageous to a citizen that the removal
of 100 dead cats should be more expensive than something as worth-
while as a barbecue grill, for example, which may have just cost
him $30. After all, all you have to do is pick up a dead cat and put it
somewhere out of the way. But the citizen does not do it himself,
which would be the only way of accomplishing the service for free. He
picks up the phone and reports to the city that there is a dead cat at his
curb and someone should come get it. That a cost attaches to this
seems not to occur to him. Someone should just do it, that's all. And
when he is told that the cost is 37¢, he concludes one of two things: (a)
Mayor Maier is getting a kickback on dead cats or (b) city sanitation
workers are making $25,000 a year. Obviously, it is easier to assess the
worth of something tangible, like a barbecue grill or a pair of shoes,
than of something intangible, like the absence of a dead cat in the
street or having a group of unemployed workers retrained. But why is
it that a citizenry so insistent upon having public services cannot
understand that services cost money?

All in all, the effect of this mix of social attitudes has permitted
two explosive situations to come into being. First, it has allowed
public employers to get away with offering certain groups of their
employees—often those groups that are the blackest or most heavily
populated by females—wages and working conditions that have put
them far behind the rest of the society. These groups, as a result of this
treatment, erupt from time to time, and their strikes and labor
disputes are triggering other events with wider consequences.

Second, these attitudes have put public sector collective
bargaining into a shady area of disrepute and, thus, retarded its
development. Clearly, these two situations are destructively
reinforcing. At a time when we need the strongest and supplest
mechanisms to deal with the growing unrest of public sector workers,
we have mechanisms that, even at their best, are still adolescent.

But before it is possible to ascertain what mechanisms are
needed to correct this situation, it is important to find out exactly
what public workers are getting, and just what it is they want.

4. For God's Sake, What Do These People Want?

In Boston, where I grew up, it seems there was always a testimonial dinner being held in honor of someone or other. More than a cultural or ethnic tradition, the testimonial dinner is a community function in which a group gives recognition to an individual. Naturally, there has to be a reason, but judging by the caliber of the reasons for testimonial "affairs" I have attended — completion of a second year of leadership of the West Roxbury Babe Ruth League, elevation to the presidency of the Altar Guild of St. William's parish, contributions to enriching the cultural life of Temple Beth El — the ostensible reasons are not as important as the act of recognition itself. There was, after all, the year Jack Connors, who played guard for Mission High School, won an award for dirtiest player in the Catholic League.

A testimonial is a wonderful thing the way it is given in Boston. The food is rarely more than nourishing. The tokens of esteem are not often grand. But it's what it all adds up to that impresses me and makes me remember these occasions fondly. Testimonials give people something they need badly: recognition. "Hey," the group says to one of its members, "we know you're there and we appreciate you. You count with us."

In a sense, you can look at a lot of American history — certainly the contemporary history of public employees in this country — in terms of a search by individuals and groups for recognition. Recognition of what one does, of what one contributes to the community, is a powerful and subtle incentive to most working people. Getting such recognition in reasonable measure can be a valuable reward. Not getting it can be a crippling disincentive, leading straight to apathy, resignation, and alienation, or it can trigger redoubled efforts to wrest it from the source.

For most of us, work is our means of gaining recognition. And for all that we hear about the United States becoming a welfare state, work is still as important to most people as it has ever been. In fact, one noted public opinion researcher, Dr. Daniel Yankelovich, finds that the work ethic is still so central to American culture that if its meaning shifts — and it is doing just that — the character of our society will shift with it.* The changes Yankelovich discovered point to the desire, particularly among the young and among women, for a higher degree of involvement with work as a part of life and to a concurrent demand that work be more fulfilling and more meaningful.

In any case, recognition can be measured in both tangible and psychological ways. The first is certainly the most obvious and the most traditional. It is taken for granted that the more money one is paid, the greater is the worth of one's work. Sadly, it is too often taken to be the worth of the worker as well.

What value, then, does the United States place on the work and the worth of its public employees? Elliott Morss of Development Alternatives, Inc., in Washington, D.C., has researched the changing economic status of state and local government workers. Because data prior to 1965 are not reliable and those after 1972 are not available, Morss concentrated on the years between those two dates. Moreover, that period spans portions of the Johnson and Nixon administrations, permitting a comparison of public employee earnings under two administrations that varied markedly in their approaches to domestic problems.

Morss found that the average earnings of state and local government employees in those years was considerably less — 19.1 percent less in 1972 — than what the U.S. Department of Labor estimates is needed to maintain an urban family of four at a moderate standard of living.

For example, in 1972 the average earnings of state and local government employees was $9,264; the moderate standard of living was $11,446, covering the following hypothetical budget. Note that no savings are accounted for.

Total family consumption	9,589
Food	2,673

---

*Daniel Yankelovich, "The Meaning of Work," in *The Worker and the Job: Coping with Change,* ed. Jerome M. Rosow (Englewood Cliffs, N.J.: Prentice-Hall, 1974), Ch.I.

Housing	2,810
Transportation	979
Clothing	956
Personal care	261
Medical care	632
Other family consumption	702
Other items	576
Taxes	1,857
Personal income taxes	1,375
Social security and disability	482
Total budget	$11,446

Morss also found that during the Johnson years state and local government employees' earnings were gaining on the moderate standard of living at a fairly impressive rate. Between 1965 and 1968 the differential between average earnings and the moderate standard of living figure fell 25.8 percent. During the Nixon years this rate of gain fell considerably. Although the gap continued to close from 1969 to 1972, it did so at the slower rate of 16.6 percent. This decrease stems entirely from a reduction in the rate of growth in the salaries of education workers: from 23.2 percent during the Johnson administration to 16 percent under Nixon.

In the summer of 1974 the United States went through a period of price inflation the likes of which it has not seen for 20 years. Figures for 1974 are not yet available, but it is clear that this rise in the amount of money needed for rent, food, and so on, has widened the gap between average earnings of state and local government workers and the new, higher moderate standard of living figures. The growth in earnings of public employees between 1972 and 1974 have come nowhere near keeping pace with rising costs. As a result, the Morss figures paint a rosier picture than is now the case in terms of the dollar value placed on the work of American public employees.

It is important here to consider pension benefits for a moment. For though they are often called "fringes," they are an integral component of a worker's compensation. Traditionally, public employees have enjoyed an advantage over their private sector counterparts in the benefits they receive from public pension systems. This is, perhaps, best accounted for in two ways: First, it is part of the characteristic temper of public employees as a group to place a high value on security while working and after retirement — higher, perhaps, than the value they place on in-hand wages. Because of this concern, they have pushed very hard for generous pension benefits.

Second, public employers have in the past found it easier to make concessions to their employees on pensions than on wages, because an increase in pension benefits has no immediate impact on the taxpayer or the city budget. As Harry H. Wellington and Ralph K. Winter, Jr., put it in *The Unions and the Cities,* "Whereas actuarial soundness would be insisted upon by a profit-seeking entity like a firm, it may be a secondary concern to politicians whose conduct is determined by relatively short-run considerations."*

Now, however, the situation is changing, and the available data suggest that state and local government pension benefits are not keeping pace with the increase in family income nationwide and that private sector pension benefits are increasing at a faster pace than public employee retirement systems.

Peter Veillette, research specialist for the National Education Association, supplied these figures:

From 1962 to 1967, the only years for which there are data available to compare public and private systems, average private pension payments increased 27 percent, in current dollars, and state and local retirement benefits increased by only 18 percent.

In 1962 average private pension benefits equaled 67 percent of the average state and local benefits; by 1967 this figure had increased to 72 percent.

Comparing benefits to national median family income,† Veillette found that in the 15 years between 1957 and 1972, the average state and local retirement benefits increased 92 percent compared to a 124 percent increase in median family income. Adjusted to constant dollars, the benefit increase was 28 percent, and the family income increase was 50 percent. Moreover, benefits have fallen as a proportion of family income: from 28 percent of median family income in 1957 to 24 percent in 1972.

What is happening to their retirement benefits is illustrative of a more general development that is just now stirring concern among public employees: the gradual erosion of a social compact that, until now, has bound the public employee and the public he serves.

---

*Harry H. Wellington and Ralph K. Winter, Jr., *The Unions and the Cities* (Washington, D.C.: The Brookings Institution, 1971), p.19.

†This comparison, though not the only one employed by pension specialists, offers a reliable, if rough, measure of the income gap between retired workers and those still in the labor force.

Good retirement systems and job security were, under the terms of this compact, trade-offs that governments offered — and employees accepted — in exchange for wages and salaries lower than those prevailing for comparable work in the private sector.

One can challenge the wisdom of such a compact from the standpoints of both public policy and personal common sense. Nevertheless, it existed and continues to exist today, even in the face of gains that public employees have made in putting the public's business on a par with private endeavor.

But, as the available facts and figures on state and local pension benefits indicate, one side of the compact is not being upheld. Slowly — and not too perceptibly — the employer is allowing the substance of pension benefits to go downhill; similarly, other elements of the compact are losing their binding strength.

Many people who go into public employment these days are still making their decisions as though the old social contract were fully in force. They are learning, as Rolf Lumpert learned, that it is not.

Rolf had staked his security and that of his family on one of the oldest and most solid clauses of this unspoken social compact, professorial tenure.

Rolf is Swiss born. His wife, Resi, is German by birth. Both are 38, and both are now American citizens. They were married in Zurich in 1962 and decided to make their home in the United States because Rolf had attended various colleges in this country and liked the university system. In the process of his education, he picked up bachelor's degrees in history, German, French, and theology and master's degrees in history, German, and theology. He was on his way to getting his doctorate in German theology.

After serving as a graduate assistant at the University of Iowa in 1962, Rolf landed a job the next year as professor of German at the University of Dubuque, a small church-related school. He and his new wife began their family: Martin, now 11, Esther, 10, and Charles, 7.

"They were were looking for a full-time man, a man who would stay there and would possibly retire there," Rolf told Thomas Ryder of the *Des Moines Register* about the circumstances under which he came to the university. "It was just what I wanted. We had a family, and I wanted a secure position. We were offered an apartment and $6,000 a year. We were very happy."

In 1966 Rolf was tenured. By granting tenure, a college, university, or other school, gives a faculty member immunity from dismissal except under the most extraordinary circumstances.

Tenure serves to protect a teacher's job security, a very pragmatic consideration, and his freedom to teach the truth as his discipline dictates, free of pressure and intimidation.

After Rolf received tenure, he and his wife purchased an $18,000 house in Dubuque. Three years later the university announced that because of an economy move, faculty raises would be held down. "My salary was $9,350 a year then, and I received no increases the next three years," Rolf says.

On February 28, 1972, he got a letter from the university saying that he would be dismissed effective June 1973 and that his tenure was terminated because of "financial exigency." The university had decided to close its French and German departments and offer their students these languages through a consortium arrangement with other institutions. He was the only one to get such a letter. Other teachers were absorbed by other departments or by the consortium.

Faculty groups at the school tried to have the professor reinstated, but the dismissal stood. Rolf began the dismal business of circulating his résumé and filling out more than 500 job applications, mostly for teaching positions but also for jobs in business and industry. He had no luck.

Finally, in July of 1973 Rolf flew to West Germany and landed a job as professor of languages in a prep school. He stayed in West Germany and taught. Selling their house at a $5,000 loss, his family joined him in Europe in April of 1974.

Earlier Rolf had filed suit against the university protesting his dismissal. In July of 1974 a district court judge ruled that the school has the right to cut back where it deems necessary in a financial emergency. An appeal to the state supreme court is still in process.

Things were still far from settled for the Lumperts. For Rolf to continue teaching in West Germany, the couple discovered, they would have to give up their American citizenship. Rather than do that, they decided to return to Dubuque and arrived in early August of 1974. They began looking for work and, meantime, lived off the charity of friends.

"I can't believe this is happening to us. It's dehumanizing," Resi Lumpert said to reporter Ryder. "We were once a happy, thriving family, and now we have to depend on the charity of others to live."

"It's like quicksand," she added. "We just keep going down and down, and we're beginning to think there's no bottom."

The Lumpert case is not an isolated one. It is being repeated, with variations, in public and private colleges and universities around the country. Tenure is being denied to nontenured faculty members who are eligible for it; tenured faculty are being stripped of their tenure; and both tenured and nontenured teachers are being laid off. Once, tenure could be revoked only upon a showing of gross negligence or moral turpitude. Now college administrators are trying to add financial exigency as grounds for dismissal, as though it were the individual's crime.

What makes this effort so galling to teachers is that the very college administrators who are seeking to saddle them with the burdens imposed by rising prices and falling higher education enrollments could have avoided at least part of this crunch. It probably is unreasonable to expect administrators to have anticipated inflation. It is not unreasonable, however, to expect them to have anticipated the decline in admissions that a declining birth rate has caused or the resultant drop in demand for the PhDs they were hiring and churning out of their own diploma mills.

One had only to look at population projections a decade ago to realize that there would be fewer young people to apply for college entry during the 1970s and fewer teachers needed to teach them. Instead, administrators kept on hiring and, worse, in many cases committed themselves and their institutions to massive capital outlay programs to build classrooms and laboratories that today stand empty. In many cases, it is these capital expenditures much more than faculty salaries that have created the "financial exigencies" of which people like Rolf Lumpert and their families are bearing the brunt.

The assault on tenure that is being waged in colleges and universities throughout the county in the name of economy will harm more than the job security of college professors. It will strip away their traditional guarantees of academic freedom and subject them to pressures to conform to community standards of acceptability, to teach what the community wants taught in the way it wants it taught instead of what their scholarship dictates. To anyone who lived through the era of Senator Joseph McCarthy and his campus witchhunts, this is a sobering prospect.

The breakdown in the informal social compact behind public labor relates directly to intangible measures of recognition. In one way of looking at it, public sector jobs are the jobs the private sector won't do because it hasn't figured out a way to make them profitable. That is a cynical definition, perhaps, but with a few notable exceptions — making and enforcing laws and levying taxes — it's not a bad working definition. The problem stems from a one-dimensional, retarded belief that money is the only measure of profit. No one has yet figured out how to attach a satisfactory value to the alleviation of human suffering, to the discovery and development of human intellectual potential, to providing a clean and supportive physical environment, to curbing the aggression of one man against another, to rendering justice. As long as we consider these things solely in terms of financial profit, gross national product, or some other such economic quantification, we will be unable to come to a more mature, three-dimensional definition of the worth of public services. It is no wonder, then, that public employees feel that the recognition they receive for what they do is inadequate, in intangible or psychological terms as well as in terms of money.

Let a public employee tell you something about public employment: its rewards and satisfactions, its disadvantages and frustrations, what it means to get recognition and have it withheld.

"Marian Williams" is not her real name. Given the sensitivity of the bureaucrats in her agency to their employees talking to outsiders, she thought it would be a good idea if she remained anonymous. Marian is black, in her thirties, and a good-looking woman. She has a master of social work (MSW) degree and has been a social worker for about 10 years.

"I like working with people," Marian begins. "Frankly, there's some selfishness in that. I go out to talk with one of my families and go home thinking I don't have any problems. I admire many of my clients. They have strengths I don't have. I haven't had that hard a life so far. I have one client who is 19 years old. Several years ago her father killed her mother and went to prison. She insisted on raising her six brothers and sisters, and nothing anyone could say would talk her out of it. Those kids have — and had — all kinds of problems. But she has managed to take care of them, to bring them up. I admire her tremendously.

"I've been able to help her because I am her social worker," she continues. "So a social worker gets the opportunity to know that she is fulfilling some kind of purpose, doing something more than just looking out for yourself.

"It's frustrating, too. Because if you have an ounce of humanness in you, you can't help but become involved and concerned. Social workers are trained not to get personally involved with the problems of their clients. The idea is that if you do, your effectiveness in helping them is reduced: It's considered unprofessional. And, of course, you can get so personally involved in a case that that is just what happens. But I can't help becoming involved and concerned with many of my clients. I don't try to avoid it because in many ways it helps me to do a better job for them.

"There was one case that tore me up, and it still does when I think about it. I first started to think there might be trouble with this young woman who was a client of mine by observing her relationship to her kids when I'd go to call on her. She seemed to take pleasure in seeing them fight one another. She'd even set one of them onto the other, and I could see she was getting a kind of pleasure out of watching one of her own kids hurt his brother.

"Then I began to notice other things. One of the boys had a patch of hair missing off his head one day when I went out to the apartment. The mother explained that one of the other kids had taken scissors to him and tried to give him a haircut. Other times the kids would turn up with bruises or cuts. 'They had hurt themselves playing' she would tell me.

"Then we began getting calls from neighbors complaining that the kids were being left alone in her apartment for hours at a time, that she would beat them and you could hear their crying. They were just little kids; the oldest was six," she explains.

"We are very, very careful about any kind of action aimed at removing a child from his parents. There have to be compelling reasons to do it. The agency doesn't want to be in the position of pushing parents around. And it is a part of good social work philosophy and practice to keep a child with its parents except in circumstances that are really threatening to the child.

"So after we got enough of these calls from neighbors, I began an investigation. I talked to neighbors, relatives, people from other agencies who had contact with her, and the policemen who had been called to the home by neighbors and the apartment manager. What they told me, with what I had been able to observe, made it clear to me we had a real case of child abuse — not just neglect, abuse — against her. I was getting worried about the kids because, on my visits, I could see that she was getting worse and worse. Well, I tried to counsel her and help her get at what the root problem was. She was not about to cooperate, and she flatly rejected my idea of seeing someone at the mental health clinic.

"It took forever to get the agency to begin proceedings in juvenile court to take the children away from her. When they finally decided to do it — we were all reluctant, even after it became clear there was no other way," she says — "she threatened to have some of her friends attack me.

"I was her third social worker. She'd frightened the others off with threats like that. Well, it bothered me. But what was likely to happen to those kids bothered me even more. The department instituted proceedings. It seemed to take forever with delays and postponements: first her attorney fouling up, and then the agency's attorneys fouling up. I spent a total of, maybe, a week waiting to be called to testify.

"Well, the judge ruled for the mother, and the kids were not taken away from her. I think that was when the worst part began for me. I try not to take my cases home with me at night. But I just couldn't help it with this one. I would talk about it with my husband. It got to the point where he was nearly as familiar with the case as I was. And he took it pretty hard when I came home to tell him the judge's decision. I think both of us began waiting for the other shoe to drop, so to speak. I knew something more was going to happen.

"Sure enough, one Sunday morning my husband was reading the paper and saw a story saying that this woman had been arrested and was being charged with killing one of her babies; she'd beaten it to death. There was a trial, but she was acquitted for lack of direct evidence. I think I'll go to my grave feeling bad about that case.

"You do have failures," Marian says, "not all of them as spectacular as that case — and more failures than successes, I guess. But the successes help make up for the failures. There have been a couple of young women I worked with who are my successes. Both cases were similar. When I began with these girls, they were near suicide: totally desperate, unable to cope with the slightest thing. Then, over a matter of a couple of years, they made progress. From desperation to heavy dependence on me. From heavy dependence to limited dependence. From that to the point where they could take care of the little decisions and even start making some of the big decisions. Now, they are independent of me and anyone else. They've gotten training through which they got jobs. And both are working on more education so they can improve their jobs. I feel good about them and about me.

"This job meets some of my own needs. I'm not entirely sure what those needs are, but I sense this is true.

"What do I like least about my work?" Marian stops for a moment. "For one thing, the case loads. Each worker has between 50 and 60 cases. There may be as many as five or six people in each case. There are always at least two persons. That means a minimum of 100 people in your total case load. With all the problems they have — these are usually what we call multiproblem families, if they weren't, they probably wouldn't be on welfare — you have many, many agencies to contact to try to get the help and the resources they need.

"A second thing is those damned forms," she adds. "There are five 'actions' (forms) we have to fill out for each person in a family just in order to open the case. Then each of the agencies we deal with to try and get resources for a client has forms of its own, and we have to fill them out. That means that there can be as many as 25 to 30 forms to fill out in the case of one multiproblem family. We spend something like 35 percent of our time filling out forms instead of doing casework with our clients.

"Back in 1969 or 1970 the agency separated eligibility from services. That means the whole financial side of welfare — determining whether the client is financially eligible, adjustments to the payments, everything having to do with money — was separated from the social service side. The idea was that social workers would have more time to do social work.

"Now, we have to do just as much paperwork as we did before the separation," she says ruefully. "The purpose is to generate statistics to make us more accountable and to evaluate our performance. But all those statistics still don't get into the question of the effectiveness of the individual worker. And what it can lead to, this federal requirement for statistics, is social workers filling out forms just to prove to somebody up there that we are busy and deserve to be kept on. That is a feeling you get from your supervisors when they come in with another batch of forms you have to fill out. 'If you want to keep your job, you'd better fill out all these forms so we can justify what the agency is doing.' That's not why I became a social worker.

"The third thing I don't like is all the things we can't do anything about. Housing, for instance. It's the single biggest need in this area. There is a terrible shortage of housing, and we're supposed to help people find it. I don't know what the housing authority does, but for sure they don't provide housing. There is a waiting list of between 600 and 700 families right now to get into public housing. Very little low-income housing is being built.

"Then there is the inadequacy of the grant. A mother and a child get $142 per month. No one can live on that," she complains. "We are supposed to help clients budget, learn how to budget their money to spend it wisely. I'd feel like a fool trying to show a woman how to feed her child and live on $142 a month.

"I've gotten used to people's cracks about our clients living off welfare. Some living! Once in a while you get a chance to make a breakthrough. There was this high-paid space engineer who lives in our county. His wife died, and he pretty much went to pieces. He didn't know how to take care of his kids, didn't know what to do. It got so bad he was going to lose his job. So he came to us for help — to the welfare department. I guess it cost him a lot, because he was one of those people who were always talking about welfare Cadillacs. Well, I helped him locate after-school day care for the kids and a homemaker to take care of the house and the little kids who weren't in school yet. He was able to pull out of it and keep his job, and he was really grateful. He told me that he hadn't known what social workers do for people and that now he understood. But most people don't understand what we do, and I don't think they ever will."

"Marian Williams's" feelings are not unique. Her thoughts are echoed by public employees in other fields. One high school teacher, "John Constantine," sums up his feelings about his job like this: "The nicest, the most satisfying, things in teaching, emanate from the kids. Old students still communicate with you telling you how much you helped them. That's the biggest reward of teaching. That's what keeps me in it. I think, basically, most kids are appreciative of what you do.

"Some aren't. About 10 percent, I'd say. It used to be more like 2 percent back in the early '60s. They're a different type of student in a way than they were back then. I think all of this hue and cry about downgrading the schools and the lousy teachers in general has done nothing to foster the respect within these students, because they hear it, too. Parents will speak in those terms to kids. This is an elitist group I'm talking about. Their parents are generally professionals and more from the political left than from the political right. These are the parents who have some sort of professional background and feel they can talk about education and can tell teachers how to do their jobs, even though they are not professional educators themselves. I think they have the temerity to do all that kind of critical analysis. But I don't think that plain people, so to speak, for lack of a better term, will do that.

"That brings me to another point — money. If a person like me stays in teaching, people think there must be something wrong, because, certainly, I'd want something more lucrative or more prestigious like being a principal, a supervisor, or an associate superintendent if I could get it. That shows progress. If you stay in the classroom, there must be something wrong with you. You lack ambition or talent. We have no economic incentives like the administrators have. And a lot of good teachers are driven out of the classroom. When people yell about incompetence, they ought to look at what they're doing to foster competence.

"I've had members of my own family and students urge me to go teach at a university or become a principal. These are people who like me and wish me well. Being a good high school teacher is not enough for them, not from the standpoint of economics and prestige. They have confidence that I'm a good teacher, but they'd like to see me do something more than I'm doing."

5. It's Impossible to Govern This City!

The variety of public employers, of bosses, in the United States is almost endless: mayors, governors, school boards, sanitary commissions, lighting district boards, mosquito abatement control district boards, civil service commissions, park and recreation boards, transit authorities. And this variety symbolizes one of our root problems, not just in the field of public labor relations, but also in the broader fields of governance and domestic progress; it bespeaks the nearly hopeless fragmentation of American government at the lower end of the federal system.

Nevertheless, of all the bosses in this system, the mayor is undoubtedly the most recognizable symbol of the public employer. And of all the governmental fragments, the city is the stage on which the drama—and failure—of public sector labor relations is most often played out. The issue that is central to this book therefore, can be seen most plainly in the relationships among the city, the mayor, and the public employee.

To my knowledge, the most candid discussion of these relationships on record took place in the fall of 1971 at a convocation of the American Assembly. It was led by two men who, because of their public positions, are popularly cast as adversaries: Henry W. Maier, the veteran mayor of Milwaukee, and Victor Gotbaum, executive director of Council 37, the citywide bargaining unit in New York City for the American Federation of State, County, and Municipal Employees (AFL-CIO).

Mayor Maier and Victor Gotbaum were among a group of prominent U.S. policy-makers brought together in the relaxed environment of Arden House, the old Harriman family estate in Harriman, New York, to explore the problems of collective bargaining in American government. What they did, speaking separately out of their own experiences, was to expose the fundamentally out-of-control nature of municipal labor relations.

Although from opposite sides of the bargaining table, the two men share certain characteristics. They are known as able administrators, tough politicians, and intelligent, articulate, and persuasive advocates of their respective causes.

They did not speak in the same session at Arden House. Mayor Maier, in one presentation, discussed "Collective Bargaining and the Municipal Employer." Victor Gotbaum, in another, talked about "Collective Bargaining and the Union Leader." What follows is a kind of dialogue after the fact—paraphrased and in some instances quoted from their presentations—that evokes in all its complexity the dilemma of labor-management relations in the public sector. As they arise from this dialogue, the reasons for this dilemma are:

- inflation and its effect on city coffers and workers' purses,
- the poor economic health of American cities,
- the fragmentation of the authority to govern,
- the absence of a credible process through which union leader and public manager can relate,
- the shortage of people qualified by background and sophistication to make such a process work, and
- the resultant recourse by both sides to political maneuvering.

Inflation

There are, according to Mayor Henry Maier, macro images for the urban apocalypse: massive social and physical blight, rampant crime, billowing pollution, congealing traffic, and the gap between urban needs and resources. But there are micro images, too, which capture for a mayor the crisis of his city. Take a dead cat, for instance.

"During the past five years,"* Mayor Maier said, "the City of Milwaukee's cost of removing a dead cat from the street has increased 400 percent—from 9 cents to 37 cents per animal—and while all of our budgetary items have not increased correspondingly, this prosaic item relates to some of the pressures on the city's budget and the fiscal

*This quote and those throughout the rest of this chapter are taken from Victor Gotbaum, "Collective Bargaining and the Union Leader," and Henry Maier, "Collective Bargaining and the Municipal Employer," both in Sam Zagoria, ed., *Public Workers and Public Unions* (Englewood Cliffs, N.J.: Prentice-Hall, 1972), pp. 53-62, 77-88. Copyright © 1972 by the American Assembly, Columbia University. By permission of Prentice-Hall, Inc., Englewood Cliffs, New Jersey.

crisis which permeates every program from law enforcement to providing sewers, from economic development to social reform."

The increasing cost of removing dead cats is a micro image of the pressures of inflation, of property tax increases and increasing public resistance to them, of public workers trying to keep wages in step with the inflationary merry-go-round. But the dead cat symbolizes different things to different people: to the city manager, the union's resistance to economy measures; to others, management inefficiency; to still others (if the cat lies there too long), a union job action.

There is, however, more than one kind of inflation. Besides the spiraling cost of things, there is, the mayor pointed out, the spiraling demand for things. From the public, it is a demand for services. From the worker, it is the demand for more pay.

Demands on the city budget come from several sources: public sentiment for programs dealing with problems given high media visibility (crime and pollution, for instance); the local matching provisions of state and federal programs; changes in the city's physical, economic, and social makeup that bring corresponding demands for city services (whether to support a new industrial park or the city's increasing low-income population); service expectations created by affluence; state requirements for local expenditures; demands by city departments for the latest technical refinements in their fields; and various interest groups organized to get everything from a sports arena to summer jobs for youths.

These demands for services translate readily into municipal manpower, given the fact that 70 percent of the city's operating budget consists of payroll costs, Mayor Maier said. "The advent of the municipal union and its effects on municipal institutions and the public has become as much a part of the troubled urban scene as the problems of municipal resources, inflation, rural immigration, urban obsolescence and development."

Municipal union characteristics vary as much as the forms of local government in this country vary, the mayor continued. "But the fact remains that the first, full weight of governmental union and collective bargaining has been manifested in the municipal area, and it is here that collective bargaining has so closely involved officials, the public unions, and the public."

Public employees want what other employees want: more. No longer "public servants," they, like any other worker, look on public employment as a job and share the same "pocketbook expectations." Further, their union is an economic vehicle, "but it has the same political aspirations of any other institution," Mayor Maier said.

Having largely taken care of their first-order concerns—organization and recognition—in the 1960s, unions in the 1970s are primarily concerned with economic issues. This interest is molded by inflation, the demands of young workers for the here and now of the fatter paycheck, and the demands of older workers for the security that generous retirement benefits promise.

Victor Gotbaum was less direct in his remarks on the inflationary factor and a good deal more personal. He remembered the eulogies spoken at the time of Walter Reuther's death after his years of successful leadership of the United Auto Workers. Reuther was praised for his social vision and his broad understanding of social problems, Gotbaum recalled. But Walter Reuther never forgot the lesson that every labor leader must learn if he is to survive. "It is one thing to show workers new horizons," Gotbaum continued, "It is more important, however, to obtain a wage that feeds and clothes their families. If you are a dove on the Indo-China war and the worker is a hawk, he will forgive you. If his wages do not keep up with the cost of living, hell will have no fury like the worker scorned."

To the extent that he remembers this lesson, to the extent that he grasps, for instance, the importance of a good pension to his older members, the union leader will engender a loyalty to his leadership that is terribly difficult to challenge.

"The collective bargaining table is the union leader's seat of power," said Gotbaum. "This is where he makes it or breaks it. This can give him the opportunity to politically wheel and deal, and to try to implement his social visions. This, in the final analysis, is where his election is ratified."

This Maier-Gotbaum exchange prompts a number of observations about the economic relationship between employer and employee. In normal economic weather society can bear the cost of the contest over dollars between mayor and union leader, if, of course, they wage the contest through a reliable system of collective bargaining. Neither gets all he wants or loses all he has. Compromises are made with realities, and priorities are shifted on both sides. What began as an urgent demand this year often is put over until the next year's bargaining agenda, if that is what the situation dictates. The contest, over time, takes on some of the aspects of a slow-motion adagio. And both sides come to accept the philosophy expressed in the old British music hall turn, "What yer loses on the swings, yer makes up on the roundabouts."

It may be the slow-motion quality of the relationship that makes it work and that gives local economic and administrative mechanisms the time to adjust to changes and evaluate them. It is just that ingredient—time—that the present driving inflation is robbing us of. In so doing, it is creating political demands on both the mayor and the union leader that are potentially dangerous to both. Workers who cannot make their paychecks keep up with the skyrocketing cost of putting food on their tables are, as Gotbaum showed, going to turn on their leaders. Other taxpayers, similarly hard pressed, are going to turn on the political leader who dares come to them with the bad news of tax increases.

Prophecy is a risky business. It is worth the risk, however, to point to some likely outcomes of inflation and their possible effects on the maturation of collective bargaining in the public sector. Unsettled times often call forth unsettled leaders, and this could happen in public service unions where the process of selecting a leader is just as intensely political as it is in the municipal arena. Dissident leaders can be expected to use the membership's dissatisfaction with economic gains either to oust incumbent leaders or force them to more strenuous demands. Either outcome will tend to produce more militant leadership pledged to get tough with the boss.

A similar development within the electorate is not hard to imagine. As the effects of inflation make themselves felt in tax bills, dissident political leaders will take the opportunity to foment or tailgate on taxpayer rebellions. Whether they succeed in toppling established leaders or forcing them further to the right, the outcome is, again, likely to be more militant leadership pledged to get tough with the unions.

"Getting tough" is not the same thing as "being tough" in the collective bargaining process. Tough bargaining and intelligent compromise are the essence of that process and the ingredients of relative labor stability. Show-boating adamancy on either side only serves the opposite purpose.

Economic Health

The dead cat of Mayor Maier's metaphor can also symbolize the need for greater state and federal financial aid to hard-pressed cities and, even more, in his words, a "total reform of the way we pay for services in our cities by linking revenue sources directly to functions, and for relieving the overburdened property tax." The economic health of his city, never far from a mayor's mind, is never more in it than when public employees begin talking wage increases.

Because of their fiscal plight, cities commonly turn to the state and federal governments to help fund the costs of labor settlements. Absent such aid, they have incurred deficits in operating budgets and curtailment of vital services and layoffs of employees. These occur increasingly often.

"No labor relations agency, no matter how sophisticated or competent, can raise money when no money exists, when property tax millage limits are reached or when the rate of taxation becomes so excessively high that affluent people and industries flee the urban areas, thereby producing an even greater fiscal crisis," the mayor said. Cities are dependent mainly on the property tax as their source of revenue, and in most cases, states have preempted other sources to their own uses.

In the division of labor between public employer and public employee, it falls to the employee union to call for new ways of spending tax revenues and to the mayor to find ways of getting blood out of existing tax turnips, a division Mayor Maier, for one, would like to redress:

> Beyond all these questions of municipal employer-employee relationships, the mayor of the large city must continue to have a major concern for a reallocation of our national resources to aid our cities on the revenue side. I believe that the municipal employee has a great stake in joining this effort, for it is also his city whose future is at stake, and if the cities are not saved, all the collective bargaining in the world will not be able to produce a living wage out of their ruins.

The money-getting *versus* money-spending division of labor might also be more equitably shared if union leaders were required to propose the new revenues needed to fund their demands, he added.

Victor Gotbaum's union, the American Federation of State, County, and Municipal Employees (AFL-CIO), has been one of the strongest voices in Washington, second only to those of mayors and governors, calling for enactment and expansion of federal revenue-sharing programs. It has not been an entirely comfortable position for the union to take, not so much because it brought them together with mayors and governors, but because it separated them from liberal opponents of these measures who are natural allies of the union on a host of other social and economic issues. From some quarters of that alliance the union has received a certain amount of criticism for its stand, criticism that misses the point and displays a lack of appreciation of public sector labor relations. The enactment and widening of revenue-sharing serves AFSCME's interests. And that is reason enough to support it as well as reason enough not to apologize for taking that stand.

As necessary to local governance as revenue-sharing may be, it is little more than a placebo for the basic economic ills of American metropolises. The question to be answered by leaders of the public employee movement in this country over the next five years is whether we have the foresight and the courage to adopt AFSCME's precedent of making common cause with the bosses and apply it to a more difficult task: getting at and curing the root causes of those ills. The same question, in reverse, faces the country's elected officials and the leaders of their guilds, such as the National League of Cities/U.S. Conference of Mayors, the National Governors' Conference, and the National School Boards Association.

Fragmentation

People who do not understand the real nature of labor-management relations in the public sector—and therefore see them as the clashings of implacable foes—cannot understand why so many public union leaders advocate strengthening the administrative and management authority of the municipal chief executive. In the nature of public sector labor relations, the weakness of the adversary is not necessarily a cause for rejoicing; it may, in fact, be the source of many difficulties. And this is indeed the case with the present fragmented authority of most American mayors.

Said Mayor Maier, "When the mayor looks at the municipal manager-employee relationship from his desk as chief executive, he finds that his authority is oftentimes more symbolic than real." The private manager has to go to owners or major stockholders, usually few in number, for his final authority. Such men have little desire to get involved in corporate management other than to insure profits. The manager thus has broad authority with very little restriction. Not so the public manager, particularly the mayor.

The principle is checks and balances; the effects are fragmented governmental organization and diffused authority, Mayor Maier said.

> Effective control of administration in many cases [including Milwaukee with its "weak-mayor" form of government] is vested in independent department heads, boards, bureaus, and commissions. Nor is it uncommon in certain states to find police and fire chiefs completely and utterly removed from any responsibility to the citizens and their elected representatives.
>
> This fragmentation of authority can also affect the day-to-day relationship between the city and its employees and can be the root of problems at negotiation time.

What the mayor and city council may agree on, some other authority can undo, as in the case of a municipal labor agreement that was torpedoed by an independent commission that unilaterally decided to discontinue certain operations, lay off employees, and contract out their work. The mayor explained,

> It is not hard to understand the consternation that was created within the union. Nor does it require much imagination to see why the decision was difficult to implement and why the union established a high priority in subsequent negotiations for a clause to completely curb management's rights to contract work out and lay off employees.

Victor Gotbaum, his presumed adversary, could not have put it better.

A Credible Process of Relationships

On the need for developing a workable, reliable process through which public management and public labor can relate to one another, Gotbaum charged:

> Professors and politicians deal with public service collective bargaining in the abstract. They gimmick it, insulate it, warp it, and make it synthetic. They do everything but examine it in terms of what it means to the union leader and the men he represents. Therefore, they drain the union leader's authority and force him to fight a rear guard action for the life of his stewardship.

As far as he is concerned, Gotbaum thinks a credible process for guiding relations between public employer and employee must be founded on an understanding by employers of the relationship between the union leader and his men. The leader's role is to represent the hopes, aspirations, and needs of the led. And in the public service the emphasis in all three categories is on security: security on the job and security in old age.

"The need is basic for most civil servants," said Gotbaum. "The very nature of bureaucracy makes for slow change. The people who work within that bureaucracy are very skeptical about change and precipitous change frightens them. This must be understood when you negotiate in the public service."

Otherwise, there is not all that much difference between union leadership in the public and private sectors. If you represent professional workers, you have to negotiate demands that involve job content and job responsibilities. If you represent blue-collar workers, there will be greater emphasis on money and related working conditions.

But it is not, Gotbaum said, just a matter of the hopes, aspirations, and needs of the workers. The leader's aspirations are involved, too. Often, he is concerned about the security of his job in the face of opposition from within his own union, which is always ready to charge him with selling out to the bosses or doing something else to merit ouster. "Management should understand this and recognize the difficulties imposed upon a new leader coming into an insecure situation," he advised.

Even where there is collective bargaining by law, Gotbaum emphasized, it does not amount to the comprehensive process of labor-management relationships that is needed to bring order into public sector labor affairs. "In many areas of the United States, collective bargaining for public employees is more of a slogan than a reality," he went on. "It can be a political agreement, a narrow confinement to a single issue, or anything except an overall bargaining process on those matters which are of major concern to the union membership."

Is the failure to evolve a comprehensive process of relationships entirely management's fault? Not according to Victor Gotbaum. Both sides of the table have, in a sense, responded to the disdain the rest of society has for collective bargaining in the public service. "We go along with their corruption of the process, we answer in kind, and refuse to take it seriously. We become willing participants in the collective bargaining farce society has set up for us," he said.

The private sector accepts and stresses the negotiating process. The public sector pays attention to everything else. "We throw in a hundred and one roadblocks to make certain that we never reach a state of maturity in collective bargaining," Gotbaum says. "Then we add insult to injury and say the collective bargaining process will not work. How can it work when everything we do militates against its success?"

An excellent example of this self-defeating attitude can be seen in the area of strikes. Society tried to avoid public service strikes by creating alternatives to collective bargaining and by legal sanctions. There is little effort, however, to find out why strikes occur.

The result is, said Gotbaum,

> We stop concentrating on the negotiations. We do not involve ourselves in an intelligent, tough manner. Everybody has his eye on the strike and its effects upon the union leader and, therefore, the union. It would be a pleasantly constructive experience if all sides could negotiate without looking at the impasse procedures, the punitive measure, or the strike.

Mayor Maier's view of the shortcomings of the labor-management relations process is as much linked to the pressures on the mayor as Gotbaum's is colored by his perception of the pressures on the union leader. Said Maier, "The mayor is unlike the president of a private corporation in several ways. First, he has the responsibility for the total universe of a public constituency. His union constituency is of itself one of the selectors of his job. In a sense he is an employee of his own employees."

Then, he continued, there is the monopolistic nature of public services. There is no one but the city to supply them, and they must be handled, many of them, because they are vital to health and survival, in a way that will prevent a catastrophic stoppage. This places great pressure on the mayor/bargainer.

Added pressure results because negotiations are conducted in a goldfish bowl, because the diversity of city services creates a diversity of bargaining units (Milwaukee has 18), and because a city council that numbers among its members men who are political rivals of the mayor must legislatively approve any settlement.

Finally, the press puts the Mayor in a double bind. In times of labor crisis the press endows him with a mythical wand of peace, which it then excoriates him for not using. On the other hand, if he is handling negotiations quietly to avoid a crisis, he is charged with secret dealing.

There are, I imagine, those to whom the pressures felt by the mayors and labor union leaders of this world are a matter of singular indifference. True, these pressures are part of the heat that comes with taking up residence in the kitchen of power. But it behooves us, as members of the community that creates those pressures, to understand what these two men are telling us: Those pressures result in actions, and those actions are not always in our best interests. What we, as citizens, give public figures in the way of latitude might come back to us in the form of better decisions.

Better Practitioners

Henry Maier and Victor Gotbaum agreed on the need both for a better method of relating the public employer and the public employee representative to one another and for better qualified people to carry forward that relationship. The level of maturity in labor-management relations in the public sector is still nowhere near the level reached in the private sector, according to Gotbaum. The relationship between the union leader and the public administrator

will endure for a long time to come. But it is the quality of the
relationship that must be improved. "An honest and tough adversary
relationship should exist," he said. "But it will have to continue far
beyond the moment."

"The negotiation process is a very personal affair. You begin to
know your adversaries. You understand their sensitivities, their level
of dedication, and above all their level of sophistication. There is the
rub."

On both sides of the public sector table, Gotbaum added, the
practitioners are "pathetic amateurs." "We just have not paid enough
attention to the collective bargaining process, the nuances, the skills,
but above all the background." And weaknesses on one side tend to
create weaknesses on the other. If the mayor cannot define his own
self-interest, his role, it makes it doubly hard for the labor leader to
define his. And in these circumstances neither can engage in collective
bargaining.

Mayor Maier acknowledged the need for more sophisticated,
better-trained negotiators for the city's interests and pointed out that
the difficulty of getting information affects the quality of the
negotiatons:

> The simple question of how much a policeman gets paid in varying
> localities can get quite murky when one figure includes pension costs
> paid by the city and another does not. And all too often, the public can
> be misled by the myth of simple comparison that does not take into
> account all of the variables that exist in two different jurisdictions which
> may affect the figures being compared.

Moreover, the old problem of diffusion of the governing
authority rises to plague the development of quality practitioners. No
amount of expertise will relieve municipal policy-makers of their
responsibilities, Mayor Maier said. And where those responsibilities
are diffused by city structure, the process is more difficult. Still, he
concluded, it is possible for the executive and the legislators to agree
tacitly on goals and, as negotiations proceed, to modify them in the
light of developments.

Politics

In the absence of a reliable and credible labor-management
relationship process, there is a strong tendency for both sides to seek
safety in the political solution. While unions have a right to use
political power to accomplish general legislative ends, Mayor Maier
conceded, he charged that they also use it to gain their economic ends

on the local level, not always to good effect. "Political action is no substitute for collective bargaining and, in fact, may actually subvert the bargaining process," he said.

But even if union members exercise self-restraint and restrict their political activity to voting, their numbers still make them a political force on the local scene. This, in effect, allows unions to sit on both sides of the bargaining table.

What Mayor Maier would extract by way of reparations for this imbalance is fiscal responsibility. "It would be well," he said, "for leaders of the union side to suggest resources to help finance the changes they feel are necessary as they formulate their demands."

If unions sit on both sides of the bargaining table, as Mayor Maier claimed, Gotbaum said they pay an excruciating price for the privilege.

> The union leader is often confounded and confused by the public administrator in his role as a boss. Part of it is of course the union's doing. Only in the public sector in our country do workers effectively help to select their own boss. If you support a man for public office, it is really tough to then turn on him and accuse him of being a bad administrator, a bad negotiator, and an exploiter of the people you represent. For the public official's part, it's difficult not to become patronizing and somewhat hurt when your former ally now turns upon you in negotiations.
>
> It is an almost impossible break the union leader must make from political support to economic adversary. But it must be done. We cheat our members, we corrupt the collective bargaining process if we do not do this.

Gotbaum added that there should be a better way. "It may seem absurd, but somehow we have to remove politics from labor-management relations in the public sector."

There is something to be learned here from the private sector. As Gotbaum put it, there are good bosses in the private sector, but labor does not have to go to bed with them. There are bad bosses in the private sector, but labor does not have to destroy them. Wise heads realize that yesterday's bad boss can become a man, today or tomorrow, who is excellent to do business with. "Our loves and our hates in the public sector are of an exaggerated nature that keeps us from having professional attitudes toward each other," he said.

The use of public relations as a form of political muscle to heat up the bargaining process reflects this unprofessionalism. Gotbaum recalled the 1970-71 negotiations betweeen the city of New York and its uniformed forces. These took place under economic conditions that promised to make peaceful settlement particularly difficult. Instead of bringing the matter to the bargaining table, both sides took to television, advertising, and the loud and dramatic press release. "What I argue against . . . is the rush to the TV cameras with off-the-top-of-the-head remarks that never help, always hurt," he said.

Finally, both men touched on the potential in the collective bargaining process for achieving needed changes in the way the public's business is conducted. Mayor Maier observed that as the cost of municipal labor packages go up and governmental managers seek greater efficiency from their employees, substantive issues of management rights will become increasingly important as union issues. And Victor Gotbaum pointed out:

> If management exerts its prerogatives and keeps many issues off the table, it is also keeping a change in the status quo off the table. The best time to extract changes is when you have to concede something to the union. If you broaden the area of collective bargaining, management not only has to make concessions but can also obtain concessions.
>
> The history of collective bargaining in the private sector contains magnificent examples of cooperation by labor and management in the areas of classification, production levels, work rules, manning, etc. In the public sector, management seems to insist on going in the opposite direction. It avoids like the plague those practices which have been successful elsewhere.

Four years after the Arden House conference at which these two men spoke, the dilemma that they outlined is still with us. The economic health of American cities is still poor. The authority to govern is still fragmented, and this fragmentation still produces discrepancies between needs and the resources for meeting them, between responsibilities and authority. Inflation not only continues, it continues now in double digits. There still is no nationwide, reliable method of relating the interests and concerns of public employees with the interests, concerns, and resources of public employers. Though some small progress is being made, the supply of professional labor-relations practitioners in the public sector remains, at best, inadequate. And the resort to political muscle remains a dominant characteristic.

These are the components of the dilemma of public sector labor relations. By and large, it is a dilemma of honorable men and of the valuable institutions they represent locked in conflict far beyond that necessitated by their roles. It is a dilemma compounded by forces largely outside their individual or joint control and whose resolution depends on the combined efforts of other elements of society.

6. Problem-Solving and the Myth of Omnipotence

Although the dilemma of public sector labor relations is a complicated one, with no easy, overall solutions in sight, it would be wrong to suggest that the picture is unrelievedly bleak. Perhaps the most outstanding example of the kind of progress attainable through collective bargaining has come in the area known as worker productivity.

The term is unfortunate because, like so many of the labels attached to what we do, "productivity" has the dual disadvantages of misdescribing its meaning and raising unnecessary fears in those who hear the word for the first time. "Productivity" carries overtones of increased production in private sector industry, where how much a worker produces is easily measured in units of tangible things: bolts, fenders, hair dryers. That is not the case with services, and services are, for the most part, what public industry produces. How, for instance, does one measure a policeman's output? Or a social worker's? Or a teacher's? Furthermore, even if their outputs were quantifiable, the quantification would tell you nothing about the most important dimension of what they do: its quality, that is, its utility to the citizen receiving the service.

In the public worker's mind, unfortunately, "productivity" raises the specter of work speedups, increased case loads, larger classroom sizes, and other outgrowths of recurrent waves of municipal economy with which they have been threatened in the past.

But those are not at issue here. What, then, does "productivity"—a better label would "boosting governmental efficiency"—mean as a general heading?

The key to increasing efficiency is finding ways to get more work and better performance for the tax dollars paid to public employees, and getting them in a way that serves the interests of the citizen, the worker and the public manager. If that sounds impossible, it may be because every actor on the municipal scene—worker, employer, and citizen—has come to believe that labor-management relations are a zero sum game in which, if one party wins, the other loses. Certainly, there is support for such a viewpoint, as the evidence in the previous chapter demonstrates.

There are, however, efforts now afoot that show limited, but nevertheless encouraging, signs. If these are borne out, management and labor may one day conduct themselves in a way to support McGeorge Bundy's conclusion that "civic life is not a zero sum game (but) a human endeavor in which everybody wins." Here are a few examples of tentative first steps toward such reform at the municipal work place:

Detroit city government and union leaders worked out an incentive plan for sanitation workers under which workers accepted new performance standards, including cutting overtime, in exchange for a 50 percent take of the savings realized by the city under the plan. A first evaluation of how the plan is working showed workers getting extra paychecks averaging $100—their share of the 46 cents per man-hour saved under the plan. The city estimates its yearly savings in overtime alone could amount to $2 million. "And last summer," a city official was quoted as saying, "we got the garbage picked up. Before then, we didn't."

In Tacoma, Washington, firemen wanted their 50-hour work week cut to 48 hours. To have bought that proposal, the city would have had to hire 16 new firemen, something it did not want to do, though it wanted to see the work week shortened.

At the instigation of the firefighters' union, an agreement was reached under which firemen would agree to a new deployment of manpower, if the city would use the resultant savings either to increase their salaries or shorten their work week.

Under the plan developed jointly by the union and the city, one fire station was closed, and its men and equipment were used to make up a new roving squad that could move quickly to alarms (many of which are false), determine whether additional help was needed, and, if not, handle the response itself. This reduced the need for manpower on some of the heavy-duty engines and ladders without impairing the department's ability to respond.

As City Manager William V. Donaldson wrote in an evaluation of the experience:

The firefighters got their 48 hour week, the citizens got better fire protection and the City held the line on costs. The City's experience in this area has been so satisfactory that we asked the union to participate with us in appointing two new deputy chiefs and made it clear to the appointees that their appointment was a result of this joint activity.

Even in big, complex New York City, where it seems the second favorite indoor sport is making municipal life impossible for one another, collective bargaining has been used to improve the quality of services under a determined effort by the former Lindsay administration to impose "productivity" standards.

For example, sanitation workers were governed by a schedule under which manpower was deployed equally among the days of the work week. This meant that for years garbage had piled up over the weekends, leaving sanitation crews with more than they could handle on Mondays and Tuesdays. The results were missed collections, littered streets and sidewalks, angry citizens, and a marked rise in the temperature at city hall the first two days of each week.

To hear city officials tell it, the process of getting municipal unions to agree to a new way of doing things was not as easy as it was in little Tacoma. But by insisting in collective bargaining negotiations on more efficiency from city workers in return for more pay, a new plan was put into effect. The changes made more workers available on Mondays for pickups. Vacations were spread more evenly throughout the year, rather than being bunched up in the summer months. The improved service—resulting in cleaner streets, happier citizens, and a politically less vulnerable mayor—is therefore spread throughout the year as well as throughout the week.

These pioneering efforts at improving the quality and efficiency of municipal services are important and interesting in and of themselves. Inherent in productivity bargaining is a big payoff for local governments and government employee unions. The former can achieve tremendous savings, improve services, and get the satisfaction and political payoff that come with establishing their elected and appointed officials as good managers. Union leaders can improve the wages and working conditions of their members and, similarly, get the approval and improved political posture they, too, need. And, in many cases, workers can get the satisfaction that goes beyond a fatter paycheck: the knowledge they are doing good work for their communities.

For some time to come progress in this area may not be as great as the potential for progress. John M. Stewart of the National

Commission on Productivity was quoted by *Business Week* magazine as saying that the state of the productivity improvement art in local government lags far behind that in industry. "In the two main skills used to upgrade productivity in industry, financial control and industrial engineering," Stewart said, "local governments are decades behind. Still," he added, "there are some very sophisticated cities and progress, while it's coming slowly, is coming."

These experiments also have important implications for what they reveal about the power of collective bargaining as a problem-solving tool when it is used creatively. Further, the obvious delight expressed by city officials (and to a lesser degree by more cautious union officials) with the successes they achieved through collective bargaining—almost like a child's delight upon discovering he can tie his own shoelaces—says something about the infant state of the art of collective bargaining in the public sector. It is not surprising that this is the case. For forty years this country ignored the application of this tool in the public sector while it grew, developed, and matured in the private sector into a useful, if imperfect, means of achieving stability and peace between labor and management. The greatest service one could perform in compensating for that neglect—the greatest spur one could provide for the growing area of productivity bargaining—would be to pass a law making collective bargaining, which is at the very heart of improving public services, national policy in the public sector.

There is one final implication in the success of experiments with productivity bargaining. This has to do with the creativity and sophistication with which public officials and union leaders approach not only collective bargaining but the whole complex of responsibilities and authorities that constitute governance at the local level. In the labor-management context, the great enemy of improved government is rhetoric. Perhaps it is more accurate to say that its greatest enemy is the process by which yesterday's rhetoric becomes the myth controlling—in a way that is almost always inappropriate to today's realities—our actions. Creativity and sophistication provide the means of getting around rhetoric and myth and solving the problems that must be solved.

An example comes to mind directly from the field of productivity bargaining. "Management rights" is a piece of yesterday's rhetoric that has become a controlling myth. Borrowed from private industry and transplanted to the public sector this rhetoric claims that there are certain matters that are management's alone to decide, certain powers reserved exclusively to management that cannot and must not be shared with labor, certain actions that management is free to take unilaterally with binding effect. These concepts go back to a frontier mentality where the boss was the boss and had unquestioned rights to the disposition of his property. Anybody who didn't like it could quit or go to hell. Well, if that kind of rhetoric ever had a proper place in the governing relations among people—and that is highly doubtful—it was during the frontier period. It certainly is inappropriate in today's highly complex and interdependent society.

But the mindset lingers on, appealing to the John Wayne in all of us. It still controls the actions of men who will insist on management rights until the last brick has fallen from the municipal edifice and all around them lies in ruin.

The arguments against blind adherence to tradition are straightforward. Why, Victor Gotbaum asked, for example, at the American Assembly, should teachers—the very people who are directly responsible for the education of children—be denied a say in the size of classes and the kinds of curriculums to be offered?

> It is foolish for management to insist it has the sole responsibility for deciding what is good for education.
>
> Everyone knows we have absolutely no social services in the welfare departments throughout the country. The heavy workload precludes any sensitive reaction by case workers to the needs of the clients. Heavy caseloads have demoralized the staff, made for intolerably high turnover, and created a welfare structure that is both costly and inefficient. Yet social service unions are told that caseloads involve managerial prerogatives. It is obviously management's way to retain its power, but it is equally obvious that it is self-defeating.*

Similar concerns were voiced in the following interview by a teacher of English. "John Constantine" (a pseudonym) is the son of immigrant parents who believed in the power of education and taught him to believe in it, too. Thus, he believes that what he is doing is important, and he wants his students, their parents, the suburban school system he teaches in, and the larger society to believe in it. Constantine's mild, rather formal demeanor and speech don't immediately tip one off to the fact that he is a determined advocate of a new kind of public education.

Constantine is active in his county's teacher association, often speaking out on behalf of teachers, students, and education. Several

---

*Victor Gotbaum, "Collective Bargaining and the Union Leader," in *Public Workers and Public Unions,* ed. Sam Zagoria (Englewood Cliffs, N.J.: Prentice-Hall, 1972), p. 87. Copyright © 1972 by The American Assembly, Columbia University. By permission of Prentice-Hall, Inc., Englewood Cliffs, New Jersey.

years ago he raised some questions about safety conditions in his school and, as a result, had a chilling run-in with the school administration. Because a repetition might damage his effectiveness as a teacher and a teacher spokesman, he asked to remain anonymous.

When asked about the rewards and frustrations of teaching, Constantine replied, "Being in a large school system, that bothers me. Now, in a small system—which, if it were lucrative enough, I'd prefer—there is more decision-making by the teacher himself. In a larger school system the decisions that count are made by administrative layers, and they filter down with token 'input' from teachers. There isn't any grass-roots participation.

"An example? Recently we were asked to administer some countywide tests in grammar. We, the English teachers, had never had an opportunity to say that we feel that this knowledge is important and that grammar is so important that we'd like to develop a sequential program countywide with certain goals and objectives. Rather, it just came as a surprise: 'You will administer these tests!'

"Try to explain to your students why you're breaking up their program for two days to administer tests that they thought were irrelevant and that didn't mean anything to you as a teacher because you had no input in the decision.

"Before this, a big push was launched toward 'new grammar' in which the student is taught less about grammatical usage and more about how grammar is transformed by use. It's a descriptive approach as compared to the more traditional prescriptive one. Somewhere, a decision was made that either a teacher would teach this new method or he wouldn't have a job. Who made the decision, I don't know; we were just told that in five years, everybody would be doing it.

"Those who have to implement programs should be the ones to establish them. One of the reasons instruction might be weak, if it is, is because somebody makes a decision then tells the underlings to implement it. That might have been okay 50 or 60 years ago when you had provisional certificates—teachers with only two years of college certified to teach—but now, when teachers are as well-, or better-, educated than administrators, it seems lopsided not to allow them to make decisions, at least any that can be delegated to them, especially on the instructional level. It's disconcerting.

"We need to get away from decision-making at the top," Constantine continued, "especially when it deals with the instructional program and problems unique to a school. The higher echelons don't deal with a particular school. Even if they peep in, they still aren't going to have the flavor of a school. We certainly don't have any super-vision supervisors. They might have vision but not vision superior to the staff's. These administrative layers have more access to the public than to the teachers in the system.

"And I think the public gets its ideas of what is going on in education from the administrators, not from the teachers. For example, the school board, which represents the public, has access to the superintendent. He works closely with the board; anything he says will come from his staff—the associate and assistant superintendents—who brief him. The board gives credence to what he says because he's important.

"At a lower level , the school principal has close contact with the Parent Teachers Association executive board, is usually a vice president of something. Teachers show up at the first meeting of the year when there is a big turnout of parents. Then, they find out the parents aren't interested in what the teacher has to say and that, after that first night, the attendance falls off, so they, too, lose interest.

"So, the public, systematically, gets whatever it gets about schools through administrative layers. They're not getting it through teachers. The only time they might be getting it in any organized fashion through teachers is when teachers are trying to sound off about themselves and their contract. And for some odd reason, I think the public places more credence in what administrators have to say," Constantine says.

"There is no free evaluation by teachers of administrators. Administrators evaluate teachers and can ruin or make their careers, but only the administrator's superior evaluates him, and he's not in the building to observe him or his performance. So, in actuality, it's what they *hear* about that administrator and whether there's flak coming from that school that determines whether he's okay. But what the internal flak might be, they never know. Teachers know that administrators evaluate them, and if they can evaluate, they can wreck my career. So, how am I going to go and squeal on him at a higher level?

"I've never been in a predicament in which I was really crucified in some way that made me want to tell somebody about it. I've been fortunate not to have had those kinds of experiences up to this point. But I've heard some hair-raising experiences through my work with the teachers association. I think teachers, as professionals, should have a way of evaluating administrators and feeling perfectly free of their administrators in doing it.

"Sometimes I wish we didn't have administrators or principals at all. I think maybe a cluster of three or four teachers could act as something comparable to a dean at a university who is teaching and acting as chairman of a department. These assignments could rotate among the faculty. You could have a person with a bachelor's degree in business administration—or maybe not even a bachelor's degree—handling budgetary items. You could get some person who's a whiz-bang in accounting who could tell you how many boxes of staples you're going to need this year and how many pieces of corrugated paper and put in book orders.

"I think the public school is an institution which can be run pretty much democratically," Constantine goes on. "The fact that it isn't disturbs me. Sometimes there's a fear of allowing democracy to operate. And I can't understand that. I can't see why a principal, for example, would fear to bring an issue to his faculty and get *them* to come up with solutions. Why do a team of people way up here," he gestures with his hand above his head, "have to get in a huddle and make a decision and say, 'This is it.'

"Why do you need, really need, one associate principal and five assistant principals in one school? Why do you need a superintendent, a director, a consultant, an associate superintendent, and assistant superintendents in the system? Our last superintendent called his associates his cabinet. I think they still have that term around—the superintendent's cabinet!"

Constantine stopped to consider if educational democracy went so far as to include students. "Yes, I think if meaningful decisions were put in the hands of teachers, they would be more prone to give weight to student opinion than they give now. I think one of the gripes of students is that they give their opinions but, it's like with teachers, it's token.

"In my own experience, a lot of what I do is dictated by students. I don't have a preset course of action, and I feel easy with that. We can kid together, laugh together. And we can plan together and test together. If you don't have that kind of warm rapport then you can't function very well. The fact that this doesn't pervade the entire school community is too bad.

"In a school such as I am thinking of, you would have people working more cohesively. You wouldn't have these external fears—either real or fictional—the fear that, gee, I'm going to work a long time on this idea of mine, but I don't know whether it's going to be accepted or rejected—chances are it's going to be rejected. If you put in the time, and you work with other people, and you know what you come up with is going to be the thing, you'll approach it a lot differently.

"There would be a lot more enthusiasm. It would be the same with students. If they feel it's going to count, then they'll take it seriously.

"In such a school, there would be more cohesiveness," he continued, "there would be, perhaps, a greater sense of responsibility; probably objectives would be achieved to a higher level. It would be like the United States in the early days. People felt involved in a genuine way. The same thing could happen in the school system. You won't have it if it's token—when people say it exists, but, deep down, it doesn't. That's what makes you burn inside. You want to say something, but the higher ups have the authority to make you sit down. That's what makes you burn."

The problem, then, is to channel this powerful concern and involvement of public employees and direct it at improving labor relations and governmental efficiency on various levels. In a few cases, it has been done.

When members of the Lindsay administration in New York campaigned to establish the principle that wage increases for city employees must be tied to gains in productivity, they knew that their management rights guaranteed them the power to declare more efficient ways of collecting the trash, processing Medicare and Medicaid claims, or whatever the work in question. They could flatly tell the unions that this was going to be new procedure. But being sophisticated people, they also knew that their management rights would take them no further than enunciating that policy. It couldn't take care of getting the new policies carried out. Workers would have to do that.

Many public officials might have ignored that simple fact and trusted in the power of management rights to get the job done. In this case, however, the managers apparently decided they wanted productivity increases badly enough to approach the job creatively. Herbert L. Haber, Mayor Lindsay's director of labor relations, in a Labor Management Relations Service report evaluating the New York experience, bent the knee to the rhetoric of management rights. What we did, we had a right to do, he told evaluator Damon Stetson. "We've approached our objective dynamically and forcefully," he said, *"but at the same time we have sought the cooperation of the unions* [emphasis added]. We've tried to gear our productivity demands with wage increases, but there's no law that we have to give the increases without getting something in return."

Seeking the cooperation of the unions meant consulting them in advance on plans for improving productivity, giving them a chance to make suggestions, allowing them time to get accustomed to the idea that was going to be proposed formally at the bargaining table.

Long and stormy though the negotiations were, they worked as far as Haber and his colleagues were concerned. And their assessment is confirmed, if somewhat obliquely, by an official of AFSCME in New York City, which was one of those involved in the negotiations. "Where there's no consultation," the union leader said, "there's likely to be no cooperation. Where we're consulted first and a productivity program comes out as a joint effort, we're more than willing to pitch in."

The Lindsay administration approach seems to be too sensible to merit breathless terms like "creative" or "sophisticated." But, by comparison with the usual practice in American government, at the local level it deserves them for the way it cut itself free from the power of the myth of management rights.

Even more creative and sophisticated is the city manger of Tacoma, Washington, William Donaldson. His acceptance of the firefighters' union's plan for cutting their work week was only one example of what he calls participatory management. Donaldson holds the radical view that Tacoma's public employees are reasonably bright, creative people who are capable of solving problems and don't always need to have solutions dictated to them. On the basis of this faith in the workers and their creativity, he gives them opportunities to demonstrate their abilities. In return, they keep proving him right.

In an excellent report, prepared for the Labor-Management Relations Service, Donaldson gives 10 examples of how participatory management works and what it produces. One comes out of his experience as city manager of Scottsdale, Arizona, his post prior to moving to Tacoma. Let him tell the stories himself, because, miraculously, Donaldson is a public official who can write something other then bureaucratese:

> Scottsdale's police chief realized that one of the best ways of measuring police potential was to ask the employee who was already on the job about the potential of new applicants. We developed a program where a team of patrolmen participated in the oral interviews of applicants for the patrolman's position. The team had an opportunity to not only see the applicants in the formal interview session, but also had an opportunity to go to lunch with them, show them around the community and discuss some of the aspects of the job.
> I was pleased by the improved predictive success of this procedure

and the change in attitude on the part of the patrolmen. They now saw the recruitment and development of good talent as part of their job and responsibility.

In Tacoma, Donaldson gave his notion of participatory management a stiff test in one of the trickiest of all arenas: equal opportunity hiring.

Despite the fact that the City of Tacoma has a large number of minority residents, these minorities were not represented in the employment makeup of the Fire Department. This condition produced a great deal of resentment and frustration in the minority community and was eventually translated to the City in the form of threatened lawsuits, picketing, etc. A series of suggestions were made by members of the Council and staff to correct the problem. These included selective certification, changing of the entry standards, and other devices to make employment in the Fire Department more accessible to minorities.

During this process it occurred to me to ask the firemen what they thought ought to be done about the situation. I was surprised to find out that they agreed with the minority community. They felt that there should be some minority members in the department, but did not like any of the methods that were being suggested to get them. After talking to the staff, we offered to give the Fire Fighters' Union a period of time to try to correct the problem without our intervention. On their own initiative, with a minimum of help from the Personnel Department, the union recruited a number of minorities and provided a variety of pre-employment training for them. The City made sure that the recruits met all the physical and medical standards and the firemen ran them through a physical agility test to ensure that, when the time came, they could pass.

As a result of this activity, nine minorities were in the first eleven names certified to the Civil Service list. This occurred without preference points, without selective certification, and out of a total examination group of over 300. I am not quite sure how the firemen did it, but I know that the feeling that it was their project and that the candidates were their candidates had a great deal to do with it. I am certainly sure that the acceptance of the minority firemen, once they got on the job, was much greater than if they had been chosen by some artificial system.

Donaldson may lose his membership in the public administration *Bund* for this kind of heretical creativity and sophisticated good sense. But I'll bet I'm not the only one reading his words who would like to meet him or, better yet, live in his city. It would be reassuring to know that men like those in the Tacoma Fire Fighters' Union were on call when I needed them.

7. A Plague on Both Your Houses

"There is no right to strike against the public safety by anybody, anywhere, anytime."

Calvin Coolidge
Governor of Massachusetts
1919

"Therefore, rather than hold seminars and conferences which focus abstractly on the unattainable goal of eliminating public strikes, what really needs to be done is the addressing of oneself to the really serious problem of public collective bargaining and attempt to develop workable and meaningful solutions in the areas of discord."

Carl B. Stokes
Mayor of Cleveland
1971

"I can't sympathize with the police strike because it puts the people in bad shape. We are at the mercy of our neighbors."

An unidentified citizen
of Baltimore, Maryland
July 1974

How is the public a party at interest in public sector labor-management relations? As a consumer of the products for which labor and management are responsible, that is, services. And what are the criteria by which the public may judge whether these products satisfy its interests as consumers? There are three of them, in my judgment.

First, it is in the public's interest to have necessary services performed at the lowest cost in tax dollars consistent with quality. Quality, in my definition, is determined by how close a given service comes to filling the need to which it is addressed. An illustration: The citizen consumer has a need to keep the premises and the neighborhood in which he lives free of accumulations of unsightly, noisome, potentially hazardous garbage. Twice-weekly garbage pickup is required to meet that need. Anything less than twice weekly pickup falls below acceptable standards of quality for garbage service. Anything more is gilding the service lily.

Second, the public must be assured reliability in the provision of services. That is, problems incident to the provision of services must be solved, not created, by the elected and employed. Advocates of citizen participation in government argue for greater involvement of the people in the processes of government. When this means further extension of the democratic franchise to those previously without it, fine — but not even the most dedicated participator has any interest in being included in the humdrum business of seeing that the garbage is picked up, the streets swept, the welfare mother found adequate housing, and so on down the litany of routine chores that make up the overwhelming bulk of public sector work. Nor should he. That is why he supports a government establishment. He pays taxes not in order to become involved but in order to remain uninvolved.

Third, if it can be achieved, the public is served by having civil servants who are civil and public managers who manage.

The public's stake in the public sector labor equation is not separable from the stakes of the other two parties, the worker and the manager. Mayor Henry Maier of Milwaukee has shown why the public manager cannot fully manage. Victor Gotbaum of Council 37 accounted for the seeming incivility of public workers to their employers and for that ultimate incivility toward the public — the strike. The list of reasons they construct between them is correct and convincing: inflation and its effect on the worker and the public coffers; the poor economic health of today's cities; the fragmentation of the executive's authority; the absence of a credible, workable process for solving labor-management relations problems and the shortage of people with the sophistication and determination to solve those problems; and the resultant recourse to politics, by both sides, as a weapon.

Setting aside the magna issues of inflation and the two kinds of fragmentation, let us consider the effect that the current state of public sector labor relations has on the interest of the citizen consumer.

Bluntly put, in most parts of the country this effect is negative. There are places where this is not the case, thanks, in part, to the existence of workable collective bargaining processes and creative, sophisticated negotiators. But they are few.

More illustrative of current practice, and of the forces that Mayor Maier and Victor Gotbaum testify shape it, is what happened in Baltimore in the summer of 1974, a summer of discontent on the public labor front throughout the country.

In many ways, the story of the Baltimore strike is typical: typical in what led up to the strike, how it developed, what each side did; typical in the predictability of all these factors. It is typical, too, in the tone of futility, uselessness, and bitterness that surrounded, and continues to surround, it. The Baltimore example is exceptional, however, in that it involves a police strike, the first in a major American city in the 55 years since Calvin Coolidge delivered his famous dictum on the Boston police strike. For this reason what happened in Baltimore is of special significance to our consideration of the public interest in public sector labor-management relations.

In Baltimore in the summer there is no debate about whether it's the heat or the humidity that causes the discomfort. It is both. In July of 1974 there were 90-plus-degree heat and 85 percent humidity, as usual. But in July of 1974 there was also the odor of rotting garbage. That is not usual in the nation's seventh largest city, where women still scrub the marble steps in front of the narrow, brick row houses on streets with names like Calvert, Lexington, and Saratoga.

The smell and sight of garbage, row on row of it along the curbs, piles of it in alleys and on street corners, were visible notices that the creaky machinery of municipal labor-management relations had broken down. The garbage men of Local 44 of the American Federation of State, County, and Municipal Employees (AFL-CIO), went on strike in clear and direct violation of state law.

City negotiators, led by labor commissioner Robert S. Hillman, had been bargaining their way toward an agreement with Local 44 for almost five months and with the separate AFSCME Local 1195, which represents the city's policemen, for a shorter time. The city team was fairly confident it would get Local 44's acceptance of its offer of a wages and benefits package representing a 6 percent increase.

The reasons for this optimism were several, and they fitted together into a plausible though not very subtle and ultimately futile bit of psychological warfare.

First, Baltimore has a parity understanding with its unions by which all receive the same percentage increase bargained out by any one. In April teachers had gone on strike against a city offer of 3 percent. With special financial help from the state legislature, the city upped its offer to 6 percent, and the teachers settled. City negotiators seemed to think this precedent would make 6 percent acceptable to Local 44 and to ignore the hard fact that the police local, with which more bargaining remained to be done as soon as Local 44 was dealt with, had rejected the same offer.

Second, Mayor William Donald Schaefer had been selling hard the line that there simply was no more money available for a higher offer. His assertions seemed to be buttressed by a circumstance that city negotiators exploited. The city is prohibited by law from changing its property tax rate once the levy is established. By the end of June, the levy had been established at $6.09 per $100 of assessed valuation — the highest in the state and nearly double the rate in surrounding Baltimore County — and tax bills were already in the mail. Even a 1 percent salary increase, city officials estimated for the *Washington Post,* would amount to the equivalent of another 10 cents on the property tax rate in the city that has the lowest per capita income and highest property tax* of any political subdivision in Maryland. Thus, city negotiators could claim, in effect, "Our hands are tied; you have to accept 6 percent."

The psychology, to this point, seemed to be working. On Sunday, June 30, some 700 of the 10,000 blue-collar members represented by Local 44 gathered in Retail Clerk's Hall at Monument and Howard Streets and by a bare majority voted the recommendation of their union officials to accept the city's offer.

All that, then, is background, as Baltimore's labor summer of 1974 gets increasingly hot and humid.

On Monday, July 1, between 700 and 1000 sanitation workers do not show up for work. Through a wildcat strike, they have chosen to protest both the city's offer and their local's acceptance of it. Far

---

*The average 24-county tax rate in Maryland in 1973 was $2.85 per $100 of assessed valuation; in 1974, $2.72.

In the two and one-half years through June of 1974, the city had received between $62 and $63 million as its share of federal general revenue-sharing. Not unlike many American cities, Baltimore had used almost all of that money not for new programs or undertakings but to keep its tax rate from burgeoning. Baltimore's 1973 tax rate was $5.86 per $100 of assessed valuation. Without the federal revenue-sharing money it would have been $6.77. The 1974 tax rate was $5.83. Without the federal windfall, it would have been $6.99. What the 1975 rate of $6.09 would have been without revenue-sharing money, we do not know.

outnumbered by their better-paid brothers in other departments, the sanitation men feel themselves an ignored minority within their own union.

Early on Monday officials of Local 44 urge a return to work. It begins to be clear to them, however, that the wildcat strike is indeed spontaneous and has no leader with whom they can deal. In addition to their grievances with their union and the inadequacy of the wage-benefit offer (the sanitation men wanted a 50-cent hourly increase instead of the 20 cents offered by the city), the strikers have a particularly strong feeling against a "points system" the city had instituted for controlling absenteeism.

Other men and women in Local 44, also dissatisfied with the accepted wage offer, begin to listen sympathetically to the garbage men.

Mayor Schaefer warns the wildcatters that he will replace strikers with new employees if they do not return to work immediately. "When you accepted city employment," he tells them, "you knew that part of your employment is that it is illegal to strike against the city." In response to the wildcatters' demands for a higher wage increase, the mayor repeats his theme, "There's just no more money. No way."

For their part, the union leaders are beginning to run to catch up to their followers. On Tuesday, July 2, the leaders call a mass meeting at which they recommend, and the members of Local 44 vote for, recognition and support of the sanitation workers' action. Thus, the wildcat becomes a sanctioned strike. The city's central labor council also votes to support the strike. Some 200 city highway workers stay off the job, but it is by no means clear how many other members of Local 44 will join the sanitation workers on the line. Commissioner Hillman asks circuit court Judge James W. Murphy for an injunction ordering an end to the strike and gets it that afternoon. There still is no agreement in the separate negotiations between the city and police Local 1195.

A city official says the city has begun hiring replacement workers, and the deputy city solicitor, Ambrose T. Hartman, says the city will seek stiff fines for violations of the injunction. "We will not tolerate violations," Hartman says. The city decides to open three dumps to replacement drivers and to citizens serving as their own trash men. Among the striking workers the slogan is, "No Cash, No Trash." Four of them are arrested on charges of disorderly conduct and assault on a police officer.

Wednesday there is generally peaceful picketing of work sites; a sanitation worker is arrested. Some Parks Department workers and men from the water division join the strike. The number of highway workers off the job reaches 250, and some 650 of the city's 2350 patrolmen say they will initiate a job action unless the mayor can do better than a 6 percent increase.

On Thursday, the Fourth of July, Mayor Schaefer says he sees no quick end to the strike and acknowledges that his threat to hire replacements won't work. He admits that the city has no way of hauling the bulk of the garbage until the strike is over. The international president of AFSCME, Jerry Wurf, and two colleagues symbolically defy a policeman while picketing. They are arrested and shortly freed on bond.

On Friday the parks and recreation workers vote formally to join the strike. Some water line maintenance workers walk off their jobs, as do some workers at the abandoned vehicles yard. Supervisors are now manning the Back River sewage treatment plant. The size of the strike clicks into focus: There are about 2500 municipal employees out. "The city is beginning to stink," reporter Richard Ben Cramer informs the readers of the Saturday morning *Baltimore Sun.*

Workers at the municipal animal shelter go on strike, and members of police Local 1195 vote to undertake a job action. On motion of the city Judge Murphy finds Local 44 in contempt of his injunction and orders them to pay a fine of $15,000 a day beginning July 7. He temporarily dismisses the city's plea to find officials of the local and international union guilty of contempt and extends his injunction 30 days.

On Sunday the disaffected cops begin their work action, but its outlines are still unclear. They and the other strikers exchange pledges of cooperation and jointly charge that the city refuses to bargain in good faith. In response, Commissioner Hillman says he is willing to bargain but only within the context of the 6 percent increase figure. Meanwhile, guards and support staff at the city jail say they are ready to walk off their jobs.

As the work week begins on July 8, it becomes apparent that the police job action will take the form of going strictly by the book. Policemen spend hours writing detailed reports on finding a penny on the street. Drivers committing the most minute infractions of traffic laws get tickets. Police cars are turned in at the maintenance yard for malfunctioning turn signals or windshield washers. One officer finds half a pant leg in a vacant lot and files a detailed report, which is reprinted in the local paper.

Police Commissioner Donald D. Pomerleau issues a statement

to the effect that he likes to see policemen obeying the letter of the law. This note of apparent praise and support for his men in the slowdown seems almost calculated to embarrass Mayor Schaefer, whose official limousine is ticketed when the driver fails to give the proper turn signal sufficiently in advance.

If Pomerleau is unmindful of saving face for the mayor, it is because he does not work for him. Under Maryland's fragmented approach to local government, the police commissioner of Baltimore is appointed by the governor, and although the city pays the policemen's wages, they are responsible to the commissioner.

Still, to some who know him, it is conceivable that Commissioner Pomerleau — who is often called Donald Duck, Mr. Pompy-doo, or The Dictator by his men — issued his statement because he really likes to see his men going by the book. "He's like a machine," one patrolman explains. "We're just bodies, and if you break the slightest rule, you're out."

Unexpectedly, the sight of meticulous law enforcement — poker-faced policemen carefully measuring the distance between the curb and a car's wheels before they write out a ticket — provides citizens with a few moments of comic relief. The *Baltimore Evening Sun,* however, is not amused. In the lead story on the strike on Monday a reporter speaks of "the appearance of a general strike." Certainly the situation has worsened. Most of the guards at the city jail, grounds workers of the department of education, and sanitation inspectors have walked out. All told, some 3000 city workers are on strike. The Central Labor Council says it will honor their picket lines, and the Baltimore teachers association says it supports the strikers 100 percent.

Up to this point the public's response, as reported by the newspapers, has been remarkably calm, even tolerant, and in many cases supportive. The stench of rotting garbage, after the long July 4 weekend, is everywhere. Lines of traffic at the three open dumps are staggering. In some parts of town fires ignite in the garbage, either spontaneously or with help, adding to the odor.

A union official challenges a citizen who is removing a bag of garbage from the curb and putting it in his car. "Why don't you just leave it there?" he suggests. The citizen replies that he is taking it to the dump himself, because he supports the garbage men. Caught between correcting a violation of the union's strategy and rebuffing a supporter, the union man turns away, helpless except to laugh and shake his head.

The news that the jail guards are out on strike creates the first ruffle of concern. But an odd thing happens. A sizable number of the inmates of the jail seize the strike as an opportunity to demonstrate their ability to govern themselves without supervision by their hated guards. They promise there will be no trouble, and when trouble does break out among youngsters in the juvenile section of the jail, the older inmates, angered at this breach of *their* strategy, help restore order.

On Tuesday, July 9, city officials are busy with Judge Murphy, on whom they chiefly rely in dealing with the strike. The judge agrees to broaden his injunction to cover all the strikers, not just the garbage men, and takes under advisement a city request to have the $15,000-a-day fine collected daily. Out on the street the strikers refer to the judge as "15 Grand" Murphy after what seems to be the only fine the judge knows. (He levied an identical amount on the teachers during their strike in February.)

The city's firefighters, who are called more and more frequently to extinguish rubbish fires, lend indirect support to the strikers by refusing to remove the trash.

City Controller Hyman Pressman suggests to the mayor and his other fellow members of the Board of Estimates that they call for binding arbitration of the strike but is turned down. Nevertheless, Mayor Schaefer says that he is willing to negotiate on the points system, an issue whose importance to the garbage workers had been underestimated by the city, by the press, and even by some officials of the union before the strike.

The points system had been inaugurated by the city to cut down on a daily absenteeism rate that was running at 15 percent. For each absence, legitimate or not, the worker would get one point. Eight points meant dismissal. As the issue emerges during the strike, Commissioner Hillman defends the system, which had cut absenteeism to 7 or 8 percent daily, as both fair and effective. The workers, however, say it fails to take into account the high incidence of injuries in their dirty and often dangerous work. And, they stress, the point system underlines the city's indifference to their problems and to their very existence. The question comes to symbolize their dignity as human beings and, for most of them, as black men. Their strike placards don't mention wages or fringe benefits. They say simply, "I am a Man."

By Tuesday evening extra police surveillance has put an end to three nights of apparently racially motivated incidents in the city's southwest section. The southwest is predominantly white; some of its residents were throwing rocks and bottles at cars driven by blacks.

On Wednesday, July 10, there is a big rally on the city hall steps in support of the striking workers. Local 44 agrees to let enough zoo workers go to work to feed the animals. But Judge Murphy has decided, meanwhile, to go along with the city's plan to collect the $15,000 fine daily, as it comes due. He issues an order attaching Local 44's bank account, in which, it turns out, there isn't enough money to pay even one day's fine.

Governor Mandel decides to step in. His aide calls Jerry Wurf at his office in Washington, D.C., to set up a meeting about the strike. A secretary, true to union-style egalitarianism but not entirely to Wurf's standards for staff efficiency, handles the call routinely: She says Mr. Wurf is busy and could meet the governor only at breakfast the next day.

Thursday, July 11, begins with the breakfast between Governor Mandel, who wants the police strike stopped, and Wurf, who wants both strikes settled together.

Later in the morning Police Commissioner Pomerleau makes his first move against his policemen, who had planned a horn-honking caravan through the city, using their personal cars, for Friday as a means of dramatizing their case. Pomerleau orders the arrest of any policeman or policeman's relative found participating in the caravan. In short, he is forcing patrolmen to arrest their own kind. The order stiffens police determination and speeds up their job action. Local 1195's 78-man steering committee decides to meet at 1 P.M. to consider the situation.

Those not familiar with the police commissioner are confused by the arrest order, in view of his earlier, seemingly supportive statement. But police-beat reporters and cops speculate that Pomerleau has come to think of the slowdown as aimed at him and, therefore, as an unpardonable demonstration of ingratitude toward the man who, singlehandedly, rebuilt and modernized one of the worst city police forces in the nation.

At 4 P.M. the steering committee sends out for sandwiches and orders the doors to its meeting room locked. No one can come in, and no one can leave. This effectively blocks the commissioner's informants on the steering committee from warning him of the developing strategy:

Rather than cripple the city with a wholesale strike, Local 1195 will strike one district, the southwest, where it has the strongest support among members. All other policemen will report for work, thus stretching but not draining Baltimore's law enforcement resources. Several days earlier the members of 1195 had, in authorizing the steering committee to fashion strategy, pledged that any reprisals attempted against individual policemen would be sufficient cause for a general police strike. This agreement is renewed now by the steering committee. As the meeting comes to a close, authorization of a limited strike is communicated to patrolmen in the southwest division, and, at 8 P.M., in the middle of the shift, all but a few of them turn in their cruisers and go off duty. At the steering committee meeting an announcement of the limited strike is made to the press. Committee members head for the southwest part of the city to view the results of their action.

Even before they arrive, the police department suspends two of the striking officers. Word spreads from cop to cop, and, as it does, the agreement that everyone would strike in case of reprisals is implemented man by man. Within three hours nearly half the city's 2350 patrolmen are out. The percentage will grow in the course of the next two days, to include some 1300 officers by union and reporters' estimates. The city will insist only half that number struck.

Even before the crippled midnight shift reports for duty, looting of stores and a limited number of fires break out in both the southwest and southeast sections of the city. Nonstriking policemen, augmented by more than 100 state police called up by the governor, put down the disturbances in fairly short order.

On Friday, July 12, the headquarters of Local 1195 gets its first nonsupportive telephone calls from citizens, whose criticism ranges from mild to unprintable. Telephone calls of support also continue to come in, as they had from the outset of the job action. Still, it frightens officials of the local to hear some callers say they are preparing to defend their neighborhoods.

A nonstriking policeman is quoted in the *Washington Post* as saying, "These guys aren't working in a steel mill. People are going to get killed out here because of this."

And another citizen, sitting on his scrubbed marble steps, nursing a bottle of Black Label beer and talking to a reporter, sums up the reason for having policemen at all in a single, chilling sentence: "We are at the mercy of our neighbors."

As Friday wears on, though, something encouraging happens: Feelers start going out in all directions. These come from the mayor, the governor, and both of the union locals. By late afternoon the AFSCME International staff on the scene has reserved separate rooms in the Lord Baltimore Hotel and summoned the negotiating teams from Local 1195 and Local 44. Mayor Schaefer talks with both groups separately, indicating his belief there is room to negotiate. He turns over the revived negotiations to Labor Commissioner Hillman and a team of city budget officials, who continue into the evening and recess with agreeement to resume Saturday.

Saturday, July 13, arrives, the deadline set by Judge Murphy for Local 44 and AFSCME International officials to purge themselves of contempt or go to jail. In the morning Murphy listens to their reports of renewed negotiations and extends the deadline to the following Monday. He then turns to the police strike, which he had enjoined earlier in the week, and finds the cops' leader, Thomas Rapanotti, in contempt. Murphy fines Rapanotti $10,000 a day for every day he remains in contempt and in addition charges Local 1195 $25,000 a day. Clearly, "Fifteen Grand" Murphy has mastered a new sum.

Negotiations with the city officials and the two union negotiating committees resume on Saturday and continue through the day and into the early morning hours. Governor Mandel is in touch with AFSCME officials, and most of the negotiating concentrates on the police strike. When the session ends Sunday morning, the police situation is near settlement. Things appear to be moving.

On Sunday, July 14, the governor meets with leaders of Local 1195, its steering committee, and union attorneys. Uppermost on the policemen's minds are reprisals against the strikers and their union. Maryland does not provide for recognition of or collective bargaining by police unions — Governor Mandel vetoed such an enactment in November 1973. Instead, recognition of the policemen's union and its dues checkoff arrangement are entirely dependent on Commissioner Pomerleau, who can break the union by withdrawing recognition and canceling dues checkoff.

The men of 1195 are fearful of such an action, and on each count, the governor reassures them. He will talk with his appointee, he says; they are not to worry.

At 11 A.M. Sunday the talks with city officials resume, this time with emphasis on the strike by Local 44. The negotiations continue all day and all night, and as they proceed, Commissioner Pomerleau announces that he has fired 82 probationary policemen who were among the strikers, has demoted 18 other patrolmen, and will not consider an amnesty for other striking policemen.

The talks continue in the face of this negative development. At 2:30 A.M. on Monday, July 15, the negotiators announce a settlement. Members of Local 44 will get a 70-cent-per-hour wage increase in a series of steps to be completed by July 1975. The hated points system is nullified. What replaces it will be a subject of negotiation with Local 44, and, should an impasse result, the matter will be submitted to binding arbitration. Workers will get full coverage under Blue Cross and Blue Shield, with medical and health benefits fully paid by the city. Other fringe benefits are included in the package as well. To the garbage men, the most important of these is that the birthday of Martin Luther King, Jr., who died while supporting a garbage workers' strike in Memphis, will become a paid holiday. Additionally, the city agrees to take no reprisals against the strikers or against other city employees, such as supervisors, who honored their picket lines.

At 3 A.M., negotiations on the police strike resume. Two and a half hours later the negotiators announce an agreeement on an economic package. The 6 percent wage and benefit increase will be retroactive to July 1, and by July 1975 the policemen's original demand for a starting salary of $10,000 and a top salary of $13,000 will be put in force. In short, the police will get what they asked for in exchange for a year's wait. Given the fact that the present starting salary is $8,700 and the top $11,082, the police are pleased with the economic settlement.

The problem of reprisals persists. City negotiators say they are willing to sign a no-reprisal clause. But because they have no authority, their agreement would not be binding. They can, however, pledge to help bring about a binding no-reprisal agreement from those with authority to make it, and this they do.

At 6 A.M. the police announce settlement of the economic issues but say the strike will continue until they have a no-reprisal agreement from the commissioner.

Meanwhile, Local 44 leaders cannot purge themselves of contempt until the union membership ratifies the agreement. Judge Murphy extends his deadline to 4 P.M. At 1 P.M. the members of Local 44 meet and overwhelmingly ratify the contract. In response, the judge limits the total union fine to $95,000 and gives the local a year to pay it off, with interest. He declares the leaders purged of contempt and praises them and city negotiators for their statesmanlike settlement of the strike.

For Local 44 the strike is over. They have a reasonable settlement economically and, in terms of improved working conditions for the sanitation men, they have made solid advances. But there is a mountain of garbage waiting to be picked up, as they go back to work.

Judge Murphy now turns his attention to the police strike. He uses the question of Thomas Rapanotti's contempt as leverage to prod everyone involved for a resolution of the no-reprisals issue. Negotiators are in and out of his chambers during the afternoon, and there are telephone calls to the governor. Even Commissioner Pomerleau spends some time in chambers with the judge but refuses to agree to no reprisals.

Judge Murphy postpones action on Rapanotti's contempt until the next day.

Tuesday, July 16, Local 1195 calls a membership meeting to ratify the agreement with the city. The policemen are happy with the wage package but troubled by the lack of firm settlement of the no-reprisal issue. Their leaders tell them what the governor told the negotiating committee: Mandel will talk to Pomerleau; don't worry. It is clear that the city cannot enforce a no-reprisal agreement, and it appears that continuing the strike against the city will not pressure Pomerleau enough for him to agree to no reprisals. There is no alternative but to proceed on the governor's assurance. The policemen ratify the agreement and vote to call off the strike. Tom Rapanotti goes back to Judge Murphy, is purged of contempt, and fined $10,000. Local 1195 is fined $25,000.

The strike was over. But the cop who predicted that "someone is going to get killed out here" unhappily turned out to be a prophet.

Several days after the end of the strike a patrolman was killed. The dead man, who normally would have been working with another officer, was working alone when he was killed, because the commissioner's disciplinary firings had reduced available manpower. In a wider sense Local 1195 was a fatality as well. Shortly after the July 16 settlement Commissioner Pomerleau announced that he would no longer recognize Local 1195 and that its privilege of dues checkoff was withdrawn; subsequently, he extended his suspensions to cover more than 100 patrolmen. Pomerleau has said that there is nothing Local 1195 can do to regain recognition as the policemen's bargaining agent and that the less militant Fraternal Order of Police would also be wasting its time trying to get his nod.

Despite the clear assurances he gave the union, Governor Mandel has assented to Pomerleau's action and, as yet, has offered no explanation. Did Mandel agree with Pomerleau all along? Does that mean he was deliberately stringing the men of 1195 along? If not — if he did want to see the strike settled without violence to the union — was he unable to force Pomerleau to accommodate to the solution that the city, the union, the judge and, ostensibly, the governor himself were supporting? Was he unable to influence Pomerleau because the commissioner's $50,000-a-year job is a term appointment and he is not subject to dismissal at the pleasure of the governor?

Whatever motivated Governor Mandel, there will be consequences for him to pay as there will be for everyone else involved, willingly or not, in the Baltimore strikes.

The police unionists have lost their union and, with it, their power to bargain collectively with their employer, a loss they may feel more and more keenly as inflation eats up the economic gains they made. There is, too, their continued fear of unlimited reprisals from the police commissioner.

AFSCME has had one of its locals busted. This is insupportable; to use Victor Gotbaum's terms, their backs are against the wall, their manhood is challenged. They will not rest without a remedy.

By having gone back on his word, Governor Mandel did himself no political good in heavily unionized Baltimore. Though the unions did not oppose his reelection (his opponent was an embarassing fluke of the state's Byzantine GOP politics), they have long memories for defectors.

Mayor Schaefer, too, has consequences to pay. Although he may be glad the police union was busted, its members are still the policemen in his city. In settling the strike with money he vowed was not there, he's now confronted with the city unions' parity understanding. The teachers and the firefighters are at his door demanding increases commensurate with those of the policemen.

Moreover, the mayor will still have to cope with the governmental fragmentation that keeps him from being master in his own house, that places the direction of one of the city's most vital services in the hands of a man he cannot hold accountable. And he will continue to be faced with the fragmentation in the economy of the metropolitan area. As long as the tax revenues produced by that entire metropolitan area are apportioned to governments on the basis of existing county-city lines, Baltimore will have to invest its federal revenue-sharing millions in a futile effort to hold down its tax rate in the face of increasing inflation.

In the "settlement" of the Baltimore strikes of 1974 one can see the seeds of future strikes that are as predictable as the events of '74 were. Typically, the mayor, the city workers, and their unions will pay the consequences of the absence of a rational, workable system of public labor relations, a system of collective bargaining and dispute resolution that — coupled with the efforts of sophisticated and knowledgeable practitioners — might well have made the Baltimore story avoidable.

What about Commissioner Pomerleau? His future may depend on two things: first, public reaction to his continued dismissals of policemen; second, whether AFSCME can make the governor suffer sufficiently politically to make him force Pomerleau to restore the union. If that is the case, one can, to paraphrase Mayor Henry Maier's comment in another case, imagine what will be high on the union's negotiating agenda next year.

Quite apart from his scandalous behavior in the Baltimore strikes, Commissioner Pomerleau represents an interesting phenomenon of government that raises an important question. The commissioner is the ultimate professional manager, as opposed to a political manager in the usual American mold. He is free of politicians and considers that a good thing. Clearly, Commissioner Pomerleau and others in positions akin to his throughout the country are not accountable to the Mayor Schaefers or even, because of their term appointments, to the Marvin Mandels. But everybody is subject to pressure from someone. To whom, then, are the Pomerleaus accountable?

The pressures on men like the commissioner are peer pressures. These leaders look not to political masters elected by the people but to other police chiefs, fellow members of their fraternity, the International Association of Chiefs of Police, and its leader, Quinn Tamm. It is these men who carry so much weight in seeing which of the "old boys" get IACP's endorsement to fill the vacancies when the big, prestigious police chiefs' jobs open up in the big, prestigious cities.

That is not, I submit, the system of accountability a democracy needs for making its important officials answerable to the people.

What of the people of Baltimore? Because of the strike settlement their taxes will go up. The residents of the city went through a considerable amount of inconvenience and unpleasantness because of the garbage piled up in their streets. And there is no question that the police strike sent genuine fear through many citizens. It looked for a short time as though the "fabric of civility" of which Irving Bernstein spoke in connection with the great strikes of 1934, indeed would be rent in Baltimore.

A major consequence of the strike is the sense of futility that such a strike visits on everyone and especially on the noncombatants, the public. At a time when there seems to be a growing feeling that nothing works in the United States, the evidence of the eyes, ears, and noses of the people of Baltimore told them that their city government does not work as it should. For if it did, their city would not become the battleground on which public management and public labor periodically must play out this modern form of war. Nor would they face the same prospect next year and the year after.

What were Baltimoreans' reaction to the 1974 strikes? To find out, the Coalition of American Public Employees commissioned William R. Hamilton & Staff of Washington, D.C., to sample public opinion.

The Hamilton survey was carried out between July 24 and 30, just eight days after the second of the strikes was at an end. It consisted of 456 at-home interviews conducted at 76 randomly chosen locations in Baltimore City and surrounding Baltimore County, the predominantly middle-class white noose around the mostly black city.

The results showed a high degree of awareness of the garbage strike (96 percent were aware of it) and the police strike (94 percent). Only 26 percent of the combined city-county sample were aware that jail guards had gone on strike. And they showed a high degree of sympathy for the workers among the public.

Economics

First, the public showed a clear grasp of the economic roots of the strikes.

More than 72 percent of those surveyed estimated that the yearly rate of inflation in the United States is "double-digit," that is, 10 percent or more. At the time of the survey inflation was estimated by government economists to be running at 11 percent yearly. Asked what percent increase in wages and salaries they felt would be fair for the average worker making between $6,000 and $10,000 a year, 47 percent said 8 percent or more. The single largest group of respondents, 35 percent, answered more than 8 percent.

More than 68 percent of the metropolitan sample said they thought that what the city employees wanted was legitimate. Here, city residents (73 percent) were more supportive than county residents (61 percent).

Of those who thought the strikes were legitimate, 76 percent gave as their reason that the workers were underpaid and needed a salary increase. Also, they chose higher wages as the reason workers went on strike.

And 67 percent agreed that city employees had more of a right to strike, based on present economic conditions, than they would have two or three years ago. Again, city residents were more sensitive to the economic straits of workers (76 percent agreed) than were county residents (54 percent agreed).

Employee Rights

On the more general question of public employees' rights:

Eighty-two percent said they believe public, or government, employees should have the right to bargain collectively for higher wages and benefits.

Asked, however, if the same people should have the right to strike, the total sample responses was 51 percent yes. Fifty-eight percent of city residents agreed with this opinion, 27 percent disagreed, 9 percent said it depends on the situation, and 5 percent did not express an opinion. County residents went the other way: Forty-two percent said they should not have the right to strike, 41 percent said they should, 12 percent said it depends on the situation, and 3 percent did not express an opinion.

Seventy percent of the sample favored a federal law giving public employees the right to organize and bargain collectively.

Despite the slim margin by which the right to strike was ratified by the sample, 67 percent of the respondents agreed with the statement that the strike was probably the only way that city employees could get the wages and benefits they deserve. Only 21 percent agreed with the statement, "Overall, I have less respect than I did before for the city employees involved in the strike," while 71 percent disagreed with that statement as a reflection of their views.

Politics and Unions

On the subject of union involvement in politics:

Fifty-four percent of the sample agreed with the statement, "From what I've heard, labor unions are too involved in politics to suit me." The more heavily unionized city residents registered 50.9 percent agreement and their suburban counterparts registered 58.8 percent.

Neither constituency, however, was far from the metropolitan figure of 68 percent in agreement with the statement, "All things considered, the positive aspects of labor unions outweigh the negative aspects."

Strike-Caused Problems

Asked which of the three striking groups caused the most serious problems, the sample put the police first with 66 percent of the first-choice responses; the garbage workers second with 29 percent of first-choice responses; and the jail workers third with only 2 percent of their first-choice responses.

Justification for Striking

When the question of the right of public employees to strike was brought into the specific context of the Baltimore strikes, the respondents' general attitude of sympathy for the workers prevailed but was diminished in the case of both the police and the jail guards.

Slightly more than 75 percent found the garbage workers' involvement in a strike entirely justified or mostly justified, as opposed to 21 percent who found it not very justified or not justified at all.

In the case of the police, almost 50 percent found their strike involvement entirely or mostly justified, while 46 percent found it not very, or not at all, justified. The jail guards' justification was 46 percent as opposed to nonjustification of 43 percent.

Reprisals

The respondents were strongly opposed to reprisals against the strikers. Seventy-four percent said all strikers should be rehired, 12 percent said policemen should not be rehired, and only 6 percent said no striking workers should be rehired.

Rating the Politicians

Whether the people of the area feel the same leniency toward Mayor Schaefer and Governor Mandel is not so clear. Of Baltimore County residents, who don't elect him, 56 percent thought Mayor Schaefer did all he could to settle the strike, as opposed to 35 percent who thought he could do better. Baltimoreans themselves were less indulgent. Almost 51 percent thought he could do better, and 42 percent thought he did all he could.

Governor Mandel fared less well. He got a positive rating of 41 percent for his handling of the strike and a negative rating of 49 percent.

One should not attempt to generalize the results of the Baltimore survey to the country at large. There is, however, a message that governors, mayors, scholars, labor leaders, congressmen, and all others who debate public sector labor-management relations should heed.

First, the public interest in the subject is so inextricably entwined with the interests of the public employer and the public employee that it cannot be independently exercised. Though they show clear sympathy for the strikers, the Baltimore area residents surveyed do not seem ready to rise up in righteous indignation and smite their elected officials for their dealings with their workers.

This suggests that they understand they are caught in the middle, that there is little they can do to bring about relationships between the other two principals that are at once fair and orderly in their outcomes. They have, in effect, hunkered down between the two warring factions to make the best of it. This is not to say that they will never rise up in frustration against both employers and unions and invoke "a plague on both your houses." They may. And the result might be either a paralyzing general strike with community support, such as that in San Francisco in 1934, or a period of repression aimed at public unions.

The second part of the message is that the conventional wisdom that has had a hammerlock on labor-management relations in the public sector, particularly in the area of legislation, is no longer unquestioningly underwritten by the public. That wisdom has held that because they are inherently different from private employees, public employees have no right to strike. This, as Mayor Stokes indicates in the quote at the head of this chapter, has provided the basis for seminar after seminar and hearing after hearing and little else. It is a conventional wisdom that too many private leaders, public decision-makers, labor scholars — and even some union leaders — have hewed to as though to divine revelation.

But it is really supposition. By focusing us "abstractly on the unattainable goal of eliminating public strikes," it inhibits discussions and decisions aimed at "the really serious problem of collective bargaining and . . . develop(ing) workable and meaningful solutions in the areas of discord."

If they have done nothing else, the Baltimore respondents, one of the three parties at interest in these areas of discord, have told the other parties it is time to shelve the myths and get on with facing new realities.

8. Tell Me How We Got Here . . .

In Chapter 3 we looked at one source of the mess in which American public sector labor relations finds itself: a set of outdated social attitudes toward public employment. Let us look now at the other source: the state governments.

In one problem area after another in this century the state governments have been unwilling or unable to act. In the '20s and '30s they failed to recognize the legitimacy of the demands of labor for the right to organize, achieve recognition, and bargain collectively. The states have acted ineptly, when at all, in guaranteeing all their citizens' civil rights. They were of little help in meeting the postwar problems of education (except at the college level). They seem to be immobilized now in the face of the growing physical, social, and economic predicaments of the cities. Similarly, they cannot cope with the problems of metropolitan areas: land use, transportation, environmental rehabilitation.

With few exceptions those difficulties caused either by the rising expectations of groups within the society or by the growth of population have not been solved at the state level. What solutions and efforts at solutions there have been have come from the federal level or from a coalition of federal and municipal interests.

Conservative dogma offers us a pat explanation of the failure of the American states as social problem-solvers: Their powers have been usurped by a federal government straining to burst the constitutional balance of powers with the states that the founding fathers established precisely because they feared the excesses of a central government. It is an argument that appeals to those who are inclined to see the demonstrable centralization of power in the republic as the result of a federal conspiracy and to those who think the executive branch is populated exclusively by "pointy-headed guideline writers" as well as to those who, by virtue of holding power at the state level, would prefer not to be held to account.

Strains of this argument, refined and muted, have found their way into the conventional wisdom, thence into the national debate about the best ways to redefine, reallocate, and decentralize power within the federal system.

It is indisputable that there have been presidents who fought hard to acquire powers of action that also served to enhance their personal power. It is true, too, that there are guideline writers in the Washington bureaucracy whose only skill is telling other people what to do without knowing what needs to be done. It ought not, but probably does, come as news to some that Washington is as capable of wretched excess as Albany, Sacramento, and Tallahassee.

None of this, however, confirms the view that the dismal record of the states as problem-solvers is attributable to the usurpation of their powers by the national government. In each major instance where the national government assumed responsibility and authority for a problem of national dimensions, that assumption has come after years, often decades, during which the country waited for the states to solve the problem at their level. They were given good time in which to do so. It was only after they had failed to do so or, in many instances, failed to *try* to do so—and after the problem had, as a result, worsened—that the federal government exerted itself.

The process by which the national government has been granted powers that once belonged to the states is more accurately seen as one of federal power filling a vacuum of need created by state inaction, than one of power being wrenched away from the states actively seeking a solution.

It was obvious to governors and state legislators that public instruction was not meeting the needs of disadvantaged students fully a decade before Congress passed the Elementary and Secondary Education Act in 1965.

The atrophy of the central cities and the suburbanization of the nation had both begun two decades before the first federal enactment of urban renewal programs.

The civil rights of blacks, Mexican-Americans, Indians, and Puerto Ricans were systematically violated for hundreds of years prior to the passage of the Federal Civil Rights Act of 1964.

The list is long, and not the least entry on it is the botch the states collectively have made of the task of evolving a fair, reasonable, and workable means for public employers and employees to relate to one another in doing the public's business. The growth in public employment commenced right after the end of World War II. It grew during the 1950s, and organization of public employees—whether into unions or associations—grew right along with it. By the beginning of the 1960s growth in public employment and public employee unionism were reflected in the growth in strikes by public employees.

Thus, putting the best possible construction on it, state governments have had more then 15 years in which to devise creative and workable solutions to this problem.

Here is what they have come up with:

Only 14 states have comprehensive laws authorizing broad-scope collective bargaining for both state and local government employees. Fourteen other states offer limited negotiation or consultation in some form to some public employees but not to others. Eight additional states offer bargaining rights just to teachers. In the remaining states public employees have no legislated right to bargain.

"Fifteen years after public employee unionism emerged as a significant problem, the record of the states is still spotty," says Dr. Arnold Weber, provost of Carnegie-Mellon University and former executive director of the Nixon administration's Cost of Living Council. He continues:

> It is true that thirty-six states have taken some steps to regulate public labor relations, but only twelve states* have what can be described as "full-scope" statutes. It is also noteworthy that a major state like Ohio is still bereft of any constructive law and Illinois has only recently recognized the problem, and then through the promulgation of an Executive Order by the Governor.
>
> The cost of this uneven development has been considerable. A large number of public employee strikes have essentially involved disputes over recognition. The professionalization of public management in the labor area has been retarded by the illusion that as long as collective bargaining was illegal or in limbo the problem wasn't worthy of bureaucratic concern. And in the absence of some statutory rules governing unionization and collective bargaining, public sector labor relations frequently have been left to develop in the dark corners between political patronage and the application of economic force—a situation that can have a more harmful effect on our institutions than the dire consequences foreseen by the opponents of federal involvement.

Dr. Helen Wise, the former president of the National Education

*Florida and Iowa have since been added.

Association, captures in snapshot fashion the inconsistency of the nonsystem of public sector labor-management relations that results from leaving this problem to the states:

> The NEA has a regional office located in Cherry Hill, New Jersey, which services our members and affiliates in, among other places, New Jersey and Pennsylvania. During the past few years, the employees in this office have traveled a few miles west and assisted the teachers in several Pennsylvania communities who were on strike. These strikes were perfectly legal. If, on the other hand, they were to have traveled a few miles in the other direction, they would have found themselves in New Jersey, where teachers and teacher leaders have been fined and sentenced to jail for engaging in precisely the same activity as their Pennsylvania colleagues.

But the inconsistency goes further under state guidance. Dr. Wise continues:

> In some states teachers are engaged in rather sophisticated bargaining regarding "union security," severance pay, class size, and other matters. At the same time, other teachers are still fighting a "foot-in-the-door" battle and merely are attempting to have the school boards sit down and talk to them. The interpretation of identical statutory language has varied considerably and all too often necessary procedures for recognition, impasse resolution, and enforcement of administrative decision are either nonexistent or inadequate.

The consequences of what Dean Weber calls "this uneven development" by the states of the country's response to the need for order in public sector labor relations has a human aspect, too.

Here are examples from among the many dark blotches of failure on the states' record between 1970 and 1974:

• The Democratic governor of Pennsylvania fired 4500 state highway workers under pressure from his party because they were appointed during the previously Republican administration. He acted while a union was in the process of being certified as their bargaining agent.

• Former Governor Nelson Rockefeller of New York spiked a citywide pension plan negotiated by a union on behalf of more than 100,000 New York City employees. His motives were rivalry with then-Mayor Lindsay—a potential political opponent—and a desire to take revenge on the union that had opposed his reelection.

• Under the protection of state law, local power structures in Little Rock, Arkansas, Huntsville, Alabama, Charleston, South Carolina, and Atlanta, Georgia, crushed the efforts of public workers in those cities to organize for the purposes of collective bargaining.

The test to which the states are put in the whole field of public sector labor-management relations is the same test to which they were put in the 1920s and 1930s in the private sector. They are not asked now, nor were they then, to see to it that the lowest-paid workers were paid better. They are not asked now, nor were they then, to insure workers reasonable, decent, working conditions. They are not asked now, nor were they then, to assume the responsibility for maintaining labor peace.

They *are* asked, as they were then, to establish equitable ground rules through which employers and employees could work out for themselves the matters of wages, hours, and working conditions.

They failed that limited test in the private sector prior to the Depression. They have failed it again in the public sector. But their failure does not stem the tide of forces pressing now for more equity between workers and employers any more then it stemmed it in 1934.

The only open question is whether we will have to live once again through the violence and tumult that led up to passage of the original Wagner Act 40 years ago.

9. . . . And I'll Tell You How We Get Home

The United States needs a Wagner Act for public employment. It will, I am convinced, get one. The main question to be answered is how much the country will have to pay for it. The answer depends, in turn, on how willing our leaders are to do a little social learning.

It took the better part of a century to achieve the original Wagner Act. No one believes that it will take anywhere near that long to get federal legislation establishing the ground rules for civil conduct between labor and management in the public sector. Change has reached a velocity too great to make that kind of wait necessary. Because this is the case, the historical parallel between the Wagner Act and the present situation is, in terms of the legislative gestation period, inexact.

But in terms of the possible costs to the nation of achieving the needed breakthrough, the historical parallel has a chilling exactness. We can wait, keeping the question of public sector labor reform low on the legislative priority list, and see whether it takes a long, harsh wave of strikes and counter-repression to force action. Or, we can take heed of our history and act to make that expensive gamble unnecessary. We have it in our power, for a while at least, to set the price we are willing to pay for the inevitable.

Why is the passage of a new Wagner Act inevitable? Because there now exists in the country a combination of forces demanding change, and they have reached a momentum that is not likely to be denied for long.

The core force is public employees themselves. They are determined to have protections for their labor just as workers in private industry do. They have reached a point of determination beyond moral outrage. They will no longer be treated as second-class workers. They want more recognition for their work, both in money and in a wider voice in what they do and how it is done. Allan Weisenfeld put it fully and succinctly in an article in *The Labor Law Journal*:

> Government employees like their counterparts in private enterprise are subject to the same vicissitudes of insecurity of employment, rising prices, accident, illness and old age. Everywhere, from the remotest corners of the earth to the most sophisticated, people seek to assert a measure of control over the conditions under which they live. The public employee, no less than his private counterpart, labors under the same apprehensions and frustrations and seeks the same measure of fulfillment from his daily chores.*

In short, the revolution of rising expectations has come to public sector employment. If anything, the phenomenon of double-digit inflation that consumes the country—when economists are identifying it as part of a worldwide phenonmenon that will not soon abate in the United States—will only serve to consolidate and fuel the determination that now exists.

This determination is growing in tandem with the political and economic power of public employees. Because they are increasingly organized, public employees are in a position, through political action, job actions, and, if need be, strikes, to force a situation in the mid-1970s analogous to the situation that developed in 1934 in the private sector and helped give birth, by Caesarean section, to the Wagner Act.

In the spring of 1974 Jerry Wurf, president of the American Federation of State, County, and Municipal Employees (AFL-CIO) told a symposium on Equity and the Public Employee, sponsored jointly by the Coalition of American Public Employees and the American Arbitration Association, of that union's determination to achieve federal legislation.

> Four years ago AFSCME made a decision that marked a major change. We decided that it made much more sense to seek relief through a federal law governing state and local government labor-management relations, than to dribble out our lives trying to convince 50 state legislatures, 5,000 city councils, 10,000 school boards and who knows how many other public bodies to devise an impartial mechanism at the lower level.

Joined with AFSCME in that determination are the 1.6-million-member National Education Association and the small National

---

*Allan Weisenfeld, "Public Employees—First or Second Class Citizens," *Labor Law Journal* 16 (November 1965).

Treasury Employees Union. They formed the Coalition of American Public Employees in 1971 for the immediate purpose of attaining federal legislation.

It is not only public employees and their unions and the Coalition that seek this legislation. They have been joined by elected public officials of both parties.

Mayor Coleman Young of Detroit said at the same symposium,

> There is no question in my mind that a federal public employees labor relations act is just as essential as a federal right to vote act or the original federal law, the Wagner Act which guaranteed the right of employees in the private sector. There is no question that public employees have long been discriminated against and, because of their status as public employees, have been used as political footballs.

Governor Daniel Evans of Washington and Governor Wendell Anderson of Minnesota, also appearing at the symposium, added their voices to those calling for a federal law. These three men do not speak for all or for a majority of the nation's governors and mayors, but they do represent a growing body of opinion among public officials who, from their first-hand experience in labor relations, see the importance and the value of a federal law to state and local government.

If the Baltimore poll discussed earlier reflects what the majority of Americans believe, public opinion operates in support of reform, although it may not be directly a part of the convergence of forces calling for reform of public labor-management relations. The bulk of the American people may not be plumping for a federal law to guide public sector labor relations. But they are saying they would welcome some new initiatives in this area. And in a country as diverse as this, that is a development of considerable consequence.

All of the ingredients necessary for change within our political system are present in the right amounts and combinations. A manifest injustice exists. The people who suffer most from it are determined to have remedy. They have and can articulate the action needed to effect remedy. They have the power to create pressure on the larger society to make it listen to them and to act on their grievance. Their case is corroborated by knowledgeable third parties. The public is receptive to their demands.

The tasks of social learning that face the nation's leadership are: first, to recognize that the forces of change have reached critical mass; second, to employ some historical perspective to consider what, in this case, the costs of inaction might be. I have said what I think they could be, but I earnestly hope that the circumstances that would establish my credentials as a prophet are never allowed to arise.

Third, our leaders must look beyond the immediate causes of disorder in the area of public sector labor relations to find the broader systemic causes and to begin to treat them.

If Congress and the executive branch do the first two of these tasks, the result will be a federal law providing for public sector collective bargaining at the state and local levels and another, separate law for federal employees.

What form should legislation covering state and local employees take? Before answering that question, it is necessary to ask what are the principal issues to be addressed by federal legislation. As I see it, they are two: First, should public employees be covered under the National Labor Relations Act, which is the Wagner Act with all its subsequent amendments, or does their public status call for special legislation? Second, what are the most effective methods of impasse resolution in public sector labor disputes?

The best response to the first issue, that of separate coverage, was made by Terry E. Herndon, executive secretary of the National Education Association, at the CAPE-AAA symposium of labor leaders, legislators, and labor scholars.

Public employees, he said, bargain in an environment very different from that in the private sector. It is one that is driven largely by political rather than economic forces, and the bargaining process is shaped more by political than by economic considerations. In the private sector, this is not the case.

A second difference between the two sectors, Herndon said, is that where the private corporation is largely independent and can make decisions and finance them, the public agency frequently is economically dependent upon other instruments of government to finance collectively bargained decisions. And, the substance of bargaining—retirement, sick leave, tenure, and other matters—is, in the public sector, regulated by statutes. In short, the employer's authority in the private sector is less fractionated than it is in the public area.

A third difference is that historical patterns of self-organization are different in the public sector. In many places the education profession, the medical profession, the health profession, the public safety profession have chosen to organize themselves into patterns that are markedly different from the traditional organizing pattern in the private sector. These groups have different interests, and the scope of bargaining that appeals to them is markedly different from the traditional design of bargaining in the private sector.

Herndon concluded:

> I would have to find that the NLRA is designed for the private sector which is quite different than the public sector. The NLRA has formed a bureaucracy which is experienced in the private sector, knowledgeable in the private sector. But that does not necessarily mean that that precedent and that history can be easily converted into something that is sensitive to the differences in the public sector. And if we simply look at the matter from caseload and complexity of the bureaucracy, it has been suggggested to us earlier that collective bargaining for all units of public employees may add 80,000 employers to the caseload of the agency. Since many of those are multiple bargaining units, we would have a drastic expansion, and my experience with the federal government causes me to prefer two small bureaucracies to one large bureaucracy.

The issue of impasse resolution, too, demands a somewhat different treatment in federal legislation of the public sector for many of the reasons that Mr. Herndon adduced.

We have been experimenting in recent years with a number of mechanisms for resolving impasses in public sector labor-management disputes. Some of them offer the flexibility that is much more important in public sector labor affairs than it has proven to be in the private sector. Two of those mechanisms are particularly attractive, and further exploration of their applicability should be encouraged.

One is the so-called Med-Arb technique. This is nothing more or less than intertwining the mediation and arbitration functions in one process and one third party. Mediation is primarily the activity of a third party to a labor dispute who discerns where both parties are in their basic claims and negotiating postures and attempts to bring them together on common ground to effect a solution. The mediator, typically, is in intimate contact with both sides and appreciates the psychological dimensions of an impasse which, in public sector disputes, are often more important than the substantive dimensions.

Arbitration, on the other hand, is a quasi-judicial function. The arbitrator, though a third party, acts very much like a judge. He is not intimate with, not even necessarily close to, the disputants. He operates at several removes from the important psychological dimensions of the impasse and looks solely at the substantive dimensions.

This is an unnatural division under almost all circumstances, and it is particularly unnatural and cumbersome in the public sector.

Here disputes arise more often out of political environments than, as in the private sector, out of economic ones. Med-Arb reunites these two third-party functions into a flexible instrument in which one man, or team, from the outside can employ both psychology and substance to effect resolution of a dispute.

A second, promising method of impasse resolution is the best-last-offer form of binding arbitration. It works this way: Both sides in an impasse are required to state their best last offer for a settlement. The arbitrator then can choose from between the two offers the one he thinks best and most equitably resolves the dispute. His decision is final and binding on both sides. Under a variant of best-last-offer arbitration, the arbitrator is free to choose individual items in each best last offer to come up with a binding decision that borrows from both—like choosing one from Column A and two from Column B in a Chinese restaurant.

This form of arbitration has the advantage of flexibility that is so often important to the wise, and therefore lasting, resolution of impasses in the public sector. And it overcomes one of the most serious criticisms of the pure form of binding arbitration as an impasse-resolving tool: its tendency to paralyze genuine good-faith bargaining. This criticism is valid. When one side or the other knows that it will be going to binding arbitration, there is an incentive not to move at all during negotiations, to hold onto everything and give up nothing, and, to trust to luck that the arbitrator will be forced to give you a good percentage of what you want, because you have distorted the perimeters of his area of discretion by your intransigence. To put it another way, the arbitrator's essential position is that of having to find the middle way between two extreme positions. If you maintain your position, say, on the far left of the dispute, you pull the middle farther in your direction and, with it, the final decision of the arbitrator.

This is not a winning game, however, in the best-last-offer form of impasse resolution. You are required to come up with an offer that shows some movement from your earlier positions. And if your best last offer is unreasonable, you risk losing everything to the adversary by forcing the arbitrator into his arms. Thus, the incentive to bargain constructively and in good faith is strengthened and arbitration becomes what it is intended to be—a means of settling disputes, rather than a surrogate for the bargaining process.

Here, then, is a menu of promising means for approaching the task of legislating for dispute resolution in a way that best fits the unique requirements of public sector labor relations.

Resolving the issues of separate coverage and impasse resolution in the ways described above does not get us far off the path of what is tried and true in American labor relations history. Rather, it calibrates proven methods to accomodate important differences between public and private sector labor relations and, in doing so, enhances the chances of success of new federal legislation in the public sector from the outset.

This will become clearer as we return, now, to the question of what form federal legislation should take. The model, in my judgment, is a bill that, at this writing, is before Congress: HR 8677 introduced by Representative William L. Clay (D-Mo.) and Representative Carl D. Perkins (D-Ky.), chairman of the House Education and Labor Committee.

The purpose of the bill is to regulate employer-employee relations at the state and local levels. Administration of the act would be the responsibility of an impartial agency, the National Public Employees Relations Commission (NPERC), whose structure and jurisdiction would be substantially equivalent to that of the National Labor Relations Board in the private sector.

The scope of bargaining under the bill is defined as "terms and conditions of employment and other matters of mutual concern relating thereto." This intentional widening of NLRA's scope ("wages, hours, and working conditions") gives room for bargaining on other than economic matters, such as the professional concerns of teachers, social workers, and others.

The bill provides for exclusive recognition by the employer of the workers' bargaining agent, its union or association. NPERC would have the power to designate a bargaining agent able to demonstrate through appropriate evidence that it represents a majority of workers. Or it could conduct an election.

Supervisors and nonsupervisors would be required to have separate bargaining units, except in the case of firefighters, public safety officers, and educational employees. Professionals and nonprofessionals would be required to have separate bargaining units, unless a majority of the employees in each category desired inclusion in a single unit.

The bill makes the question of a union shop (in which union membership is a condition of employment) a bargainable item. Absent a union shop, an agency shop is mandated in which each employee in the bargaining unit must pay an agency shop fee equal to the dues, fees, and assessments that a member of the union or association is charged.

Thus, there can be a union shop if it is negotiated, but the union or association is guarded against the financial risks of an agency shop. Since all employees, whether or not they belong to the union, benefit from its representational activities, it is only fair they should pay the freight.

The section dealing with procedures for resolving impasses contains some of the most important of the bill's provisions. These aim at permitting elected officials, who are ultimately the management, as well as employee representatives to demonstrate to the public that they have left no stone unturned in an effort to reach agreement prior to a strike.

To accomplish this end, the bill provides mediative and fact-finding machinery with fixed time limits, so that disputes can be expedited and the parties, on entering negotiations, know the specific time constraints with which they are confronted.

Time is important, because in public sector bargaining the interlocking relationship of the various strata of government—particularly with regard to budget matters—requires that third-party intervention, if it is to be of help, be utilized in time.

Under the bill, either party or the Federal Mediation and Conciliation Service may declare an impasse to exist. Should the service decide that an impasse does exist, it would appoint a mediator who would have 15 days to try to bring the parties to agreement. Should the mediator fail, either party may request fact-finding, the fact-finder to be selected by the parties or, failing agreement among them, by the service.

At this point the bill would provide a new procedure that would allow for an optional alternative to the strike. Within five days of requesting (or receiving a request for) fact-finding, the employee representative must opt to enter either binding arbitration of the issues or retain the right to strike, should the fact-finder's recommendations be unacceptable. Under this procedure the inherent right of any employee to strike is not infringed, while an alternative to a possible strike is available.

The employee organization stakes its all on its decision to opt for binding arbitration or a possible strike. The public agency, on the other hand, still retains the right to seek injunctive relief should a strike occur. This concept has undergone extensive testing in Canada's public sector labor relations. The idea of giving employees their choice of dispute-resolving mechanisms originated as a legislative compromise between one group of Canadian workers averse to using the strike tool and another that strongly objected to passage of the ground-breaking Public Service Staff Relations Act without a strike provision. As it has worked out, according to Jake Finkelman, chairman of the Public Services Staff Relations Board that oversees the act, giving organizations the right to choose has resulted in the majority of units opting for arbitration over the right to strike.

Clay-Perkins defines unfair labor practices for both management and labor and empowers NPERC to prevent them. For an employer it would be unlawful to:

- make reprisals or discriminate against an employee for exercising his rights under the statute;
- dominate or interfere with the formation or administration of an employee organization;
- encourage or discourage membership in an employee organization by discriminating in regard to hire, tenure, or other terms and conditions of employment;
- fail to bargain in good faith with a recognized organization;
- deny an employee organization a place to meet, access to work areas, bulletin boards, and mailboxes; or
- refuse to deduct from employees' wages membership dues for employee organizations or to grant dues deduction rights to any organization other than the exclusive representative.

For an employee organization it would be unlawful to:

- attempt to cause an employer to commit an act prohibited by statute;
- restrain or coerce an employee in the exercise of the rights guaranteed by the statute or an employer in the selection of its bargaining representatives; or
- fail to bargain in good faith if it has been recognized as the exclusive representative.

This, in my view and the view of the leaders of the organizations that are members of the Coalition of American Public Employees, is the kind of Wagner Act for public employment that the country needs.

The Coalition favors separate but parallel legislation to extend collective bargaining rights to 3 million federal workers: The preferable legislation, introduced by Representative William Ford of Michigan in the last Congress, is parallel because the concerns of federal employees are much the same as those of their state and local counterparts. It must be separate, however, because of the unique role that Congress plays in the federal employer-employee relationship. There is a strong and longstanding tradition of close congressional oversight of laws, budgets, and regulations affecting federal employees. Furthermore, this oversight traditionally has been removed from the jurisdiction of those subcommittees in both houses that deal with general labor problems and policies and given, instead, to the committees that regulate the postal service and civil service. Substantively, however, all the arguments in favor of Clay-Perkins are also arguments in favor of the Ford Bill.

There are other proposals for extending a federal guarantee of collective bargaining rights to state and local public employees. Three of them merit close attention.

The first calls for legislation creating a federal-state partnership to regulate public sector labor relations. Under this proposal Congress would define the basic rules governing labor-management relations, and the executive would retain a reserve administrative authority over the enforcement of those rules but permit the states discretion to implement the rules and experiment with different policies in important substantive areas, such as defining what comprises a bargaining unit and the whole area of impasse resolution.

The basic rules would be these: Employees would have a right to organize and engage in collective bargaining. They would have a right to join or not join a union. Unfair labor practices by employers and unions would be defined. Election procedures would be established for orderly solution of disputes over questions of representation. Adoption of the concept of an exclusive bargaining agent would be mandatory. There would be procedural requirements for bargaining in good faith.

Any state with a law in substantial conformity with these federally set standards would be given authority to administer its own legal provisions without direct federal intervention but subject to periodic federal review.

The federal law would apply in cases where states failed to enact conforming laws or adopted nonconforming statutes, and a special Public Employee Relations Board would be established to exercise this reserve authority. In any case, a state would be free to develop rules and procedures related to collective bargaining and to the resolution of impasses. States with conforming laws would be free to make unit determinations, that is, define the bargaining unit.

This proposal enjoys the sponsorship and advocacy of, among other distinguished men, Arvid Anderson, chairman of the Office of Collective Bargaining in New York City, and Arnold R. Weber, provost of Carnegie-Mellon University.

Dean Weber, speaking to the CAPE-AAA symposium, made this case for the federal-state approach:

> It attempts to separate the question of affording public employees the basic rights of representation from the more diverse issues of bargaining structure, tactics, and substance. It also permits the state to engage in wide experimentation without indulging the fancy that forty years of private sector experience is somehow grandly irrelevant.
>
> This "standards" approach has been used by a few states in relating state public bargaining laws to municipal situations and should not be either uncongenial or unfamiliar when applied one level higher in the structure of American government.
>
> Labor-management relations in the public sector are slowly edging toward maturity in the United States and have entered a crucial stage in their development. The stakes in terms of public order and public efficiency are high. The public sector unions are now sufficiently strong so that they are unlikely to accept what appears to be a capricious distribution of rights. The federal government should not be—and as a practical matter cannot be—aloof from the way this controversy is resolved. If the states are indeed sources of experimentation and innovation they will turn these attributes to the forging of a constructive federal-state partnership.

The state-federal approach is worthy on several counts. First, it satisfies the criterion of separate coverage. Second, it is a masterful compromise of contending interests, which should allay fears, *on the employer side*, of a total federal takeover in this field. Such fears have their political consequences, for, in a number of states, there are strong public sector labor relations agencies that over the years have built up considerable political muscle within their own congressional delegations and in Congress generally. These agencies will arm themselves against a straight federal law, and the approach advocated by Anderson and Weber is, no doubt, designed with their potential opposition in mind.

This approach has a number of weaknesses, too. Not the least of them is its failure to address fears on the *employee* side of the question. This fear appears to some to revolve around the issue of experimentation and innovation. That is not the case, and it is unfortunate that public employees and their unions are cast as opposing new departures in a field that so clearly needs them. Their fear is not of new initiatives but of the consequences of assigning responsibility for them to the states. Dean Weber assures us, "If the states are indeed sources of experimentation and innovation, they will turn these attributes to the forging of a constructive federal-state partnership."

But what if they are not and will not? This is a very serious question in the minds of public employees and their leaders. Their experience with the willingness of state governments to be fair, let alone to experiment constructively, in search of better labor relations is long, first-hand, and, by and large, dismal. No amount of rhetoric about a new federalism in which states assume a forward-looking visage is likely to wipe out the memory of what they have been through at the hands of state legislators, governors, and other officials. Nor will rhetoric lead them to master their fear of entrusting the future welfare of public sector labor relations to the likes of men who compiled such an unattractive record in this area. Public employees have good reason to be skeptical of the wisdom of establishing state governments as benign arbiters of public sector labor relations, just as the union men and women of the 1930s were skeptical of the notion that the Weirton steels and Budd manufacturings of the country would voluntarily act to establish the principle of equity in private sector labor relations.

A second failing of the federal-state approach in its present form is the minimal attention it gives to the second of the two criteria questions mentioned earlier: Which are the most effective methods of impasse resolution in public sector labor disputes? Again, the disquiet that public employees are likely to feel with this weakness stems not from an opposition to innovative experimentation with impasse-resolving mechanisms. Rather, it arises from the proposal's excessive pluralism and its undocumented faith that state governments will be disposed to experiment and innovate in this area. It is likely that, absent a federal requirement to seek new mechanisms, most states would shirk the difficult and often troublesome duties involved in such a search.

There is a third disturbing weakness in this approach: its failure to be concerned with questions of consistency in the development of precedent. To have various states controlling implementation of federal standards would, very likely, mean having variations in policy from state to state on such important matters as unit recognition and the finer questions involved in applying unfair labor practices standards, to give two examples. This would make for uneven, lumpy growth in the body of law that will arise from rulings, interpretations, and decisions at the state level. At the end of a decade we could end up with federally sanctioned law being, in practice, significantly different in New Jersey than in, say, Ohio. In other words we could well spend a decade getting back to the point at which matters are today in the public sector.

In this case it is not a foolish consistency that is at issue. There are instructive parallels to consider. Workmen's compensation, for example, came into being under the Social Security Act with a provision for preemption of administration by the states, an option that was exercised. The net effect has been that workmen's "comp" is totally the province of the states. The federal government is effectively excluded from its operation. This has caused substantial problems, not the least of which is that American workers in one state get far less in the way of compensation than do workers in another, despite the fact that both are covered by a single federal law and paid, in the main, with federal money. Nor can these inconsistencies in coverage be said to result solely from variations from state to state in local economies and living standards.

Something similar seems to be happening with the federal Occupational Safety and Health Act, administration of which has been given to the states. At present there is a nationwide clamor for more consistency in the application of this federal law. Part of the problem seems to be that Congress failed to appropriate funds for federal policing of state administration.

While the federal-state approach is clearly a second choice to the approach embodied in the Clay-Perkins bill, it is one of those second choices that could, with proper attention, be upgraded, should the vicissitudes of legislative life make such an effort necessary.

If the federal-state approach just discussed suffers from too much pluralism, the third major proposal for regulating public sector labor relations—simple amendment of the National Labor Relations Act to cover state and local workers—suffers from too much rigidity. It has two things to its credit: It would be the easiest of the three models to erect and set running, and it would insure nationwide consistency in the administration of the law.

The most serious fault to be found with covering public employees under NLRA, however, is that it does not deal with two basic facts:

- public employment and public employees are different from private employment and private employees;
- public employees need, in their relations with their jobs and their bosses, to be treated as different.

The differences may not seem great, but, in terms of both the public interest and the interest of public employees, recognizing them is vital, for reasons that Terry Herndon covered in remarks quoted earlier in this chapter.

To come under the National Labor Relations Act means to come under the National Labor Relations Board. The board is an institution freighted with 40 years of judicial and quasi-judicial decisions and precedents. These represent, in themselves, a body of law evolved to meet specific situations in the private sector during a period of economic history that no longer exists. If this means that much of this body of law is out of date in the sector it regulates, then consider how much more inapplicable it is to the public sector.

Let me illustrate with an example in the form of another serious objection to this approach. The private sector's—and, thus, the NLRB's—cut-and-dried definition of what constitutes a supervisor creates problems for public labor relations. Private-sector unions long have had a legitimate concern that supervisors, who are direct representatives of management, be foreclosed from membership in their union and participation in its affairs. In the public sector, on the other hand, the definition of who is or is not a supervisor needs to be made with the subtlety and flexibility that reality dictates. The reality is that there are many public employees who hold fancy titles but have no substantive power over their fellow employees and little affiliation with the interests of management. To treat them as supervisors in the NLRA meaning of that term would be ludicrous and unfair. It would, in fact, deny many employees deserving of union membership and representation the benefits of both and create inequity in the name of correcting it.

The NLRA-NLRB approach has the further disadvantage of wiping out the statutory benefits that public employees have won from state governments, such as tenure acts and retirement systems. Further, simple extension of NLRA to the public sector does nothing about the prosaic, but very real, problem of staffing NLRB adequately to handle a new constituency of 10 million state and local employees. The board's existing resources are strained just taking care of its private sector responsibilities. Without a substantial increase in its capacity, NLRB would be forced to give second-priority attention to public sector labor relations at the outset of coverage, when they would need its most careful attention.

Manifestly failing to meet the first of the two criteria for good legislation, the NLRA-NLRB approach also fails to meet public employment's needs for effective methods of dispute resolution, disputes that are, more often than not, different from the disputes that arise in the private sector.

The extent of the difference can be understood by looking at the issues over which teachers struck in the 1974-75 school year. Not surprisingly, in a time of rampant inflation, one of the leading issues was wages. In this, teachers and other public employees are at one with their private sector colleagues. But look at the other four leading issues: class size, a voice in budget planning, additional teaching staff, and better grievance procedures. These are not the kinds of issues over which workers in the private sector struck in the same period.

This should not be read as an argument that public workers are inherently different people from private workers, that they are better, finer, more sensitive souls. Instead, it should be read for what it is: evidence that the kind of work done by most public employees creates, by its very difference from manufacturing, extracting, farming, or what have you, different problems for the workers. These problems dictate, in turn, a different set of issues over which public employees, in my experience an essentially conservative class of people, are willing to go to the extreme of a strike. Understanding this, it should not be hard to understand these corollaries:

- The means of resolving disputes and strikes should be different from those used in the private sector if they are to be effective.
- These differences require a different approach to collective bargaining itself and, indeed, to the whole process of labor-management relations than is followed in the private sector.
- Finally, these considerations justify passage of federal collective bargaining legislation that accomodates these important differences and, thus, better fits the conditions it addresses.

The third alternative is to retain coverage of public employees under the National Labor Relations Act but to so substantively amend the act that the major differences between the public and private sectors are accommodated. Retaining the shell of NLRA coverage while, in effect, providing separate legislation for public employees has the advantage of providing needed change while retaining the illusion of minor adjustment. This kind of game-playing may seem silly; but it may be necessary to effect the legislative consensus required to pass a law.

The precise form that legislation ultimately takes is not an ideological sticking point for the Coalition of American Public Employees or most of the other organizations and individuals who support the principles of the Clay-Perkins bill. We are primarily concerned about getting coverage and getting the most suitable coverage we can, in that order. We are not interested in engaging in a triumph of legislative technique over purpose. We can conceive of the principles—or most of the principles—of Clay-Perkins being incorporated without fatal injury into the form of either an extremely amended NLRA or the state-federal approaches. Just as we have sought to avoid a Simon-pure posture in our legislative advocacy, we expect as much of others who advocate approaches different from our own. Achieving an acceptable compromise will demand not only concessions but creative and imaginative thinking.

Congress is fast approaching the point of deciding whether it will timidly opt for business as usual or seek to chart a new and admittedly more difficult course. The organizations that represent the majority of organized public workers, whether members of the Coalition or not, urge Congress to be bold. The AFL-CIO, on the other hand, urges them to be timid. It opts for the pure-and-simple NLRA-NLRB approach. This decision is regrettable, for, among other things, it means that their considerable influence with Congress in the field of labor legislation will be pitted against the Coalition and its allies in the fight for the best possible public sector law and the best compromise legislation when the need for compromise comes, as it surely will. Regrettable as it is, it also is understandable.

The AFL-CIO is dominated by private sector unions that have shown little interest in or sympathy with public sector unions or workers. Old-line union leaders continue to think of themselves as the "heavies" of organized labor and of the leaders of public sector organizations as lightweights (although the "lightweights" built and preside over the only labor organizations inside or outside AFL-CIO whose membership increases, while private sector unions decline or barely hold even). This attitude may account for the fact that it was not until late 1974 that the federation created a public employees department, raising public employees to at least symbolic equivalence within its hierarchy with workers in, say, the building trades and maritime occupations. Private sector domination of the federation also warps its decision-making process. In order to take any stand at all on the question of federal legislation of public sector collective bargaining, the federation had to seek a consensus suitable to the craft and industrial unions. As it has before, this constraint led AFL-CIO to settle on the lowest common denominator, the simplistic NLRA-NLRB approach. This requirement also produced some ironic twists! First, the AFL-CIO position is diametrically opposed to that held by the two largest public employee unions within the AFL-CIO—AFSCME and the International Association of Firefighters—both of which strongly endorse the Clay-Perkins approach. Another irony is that, while AFL-CIO rests much of its case for NLRA-NLRB on the argument that organized labor should be covered by one and the same law, it has, inconsistently, opted for separate coverage of federal employees.

It is understandable, too, that the AFL-CIO position on public sector collective bargaining is influenced by its long-standing emotional and institutional allegiances to the National Labor Relations Act and the National Labor Relations Board. Many of the men who control AFL-CIO today fought hard for the Wagner Act when they were young labor leaders. In the intervening 40 years they and their unions have become accustomed to and comfortable with it. They know how the law and the board work and how to use both to their advantage. Their satisfaction is evidenced by the fact that, despite the sweeping changes in our society, the American economy, and the needs of the American work force over those four decades, the AFL-CIO leadership has rarely sought changes in NLRA. And they sincerely do not understand why something that has served the labor hierarchy so well is not acceptable to everyone in the labor movement. Nor do they understand why the men and women of the public sector give them the following explanation:

Being forced into the private sector mold by a straightaway NLRA-NLRB law would tend to chill, depress, and postpone creative and innovative responses to the issues that matter to our members, to us, and to the larger society: impasse resolution, productivity bargaining, improving the quality of working life, building participatory decision-making at the work place. Being forced into the private sector mold without regard to the principles embodied in Clay-Perkins would betray people like the teacher, "John Constantine," people who desire to create through collective bargaining better and more humane ways of doing their jobs. It would betray public officials like William Donaldson, the Tacoma city manager, in their pioneering efforts to improve labor-management relations and, with them, municipal efficiency. Being forced into the pure-and-simple private sector mold would betray all of us as citizens and taxpayers whose interests are served by fostering better ways of doing the public business and achieving equitable treatment of public workers.

Our answer, in short, is that the lowest common denominator is not good enough for us, for the American labor movement, or for the American people.

10. A New Kind of Management, A New Kind of Labor

Anyone who advocates passage of legislation such as the Clay-Perkins bill must be exact in his claims for its efficacy, explicit in his expectations for what such a law will and will not do. It will not be a cure-all for the problems imposed on employees, employers, and citizens by the forces at work in the public sector, any more than the original Wagner Act healed the ailing body of private sector labor-management relations overnight. Achieving such a law is not the only item on the agenda of reform. It *is* a necessary first step for bringing order into an increasingly disordered and troublesome phase of our common national life.

A Clay-Perkins bill will not abolish strikes. Rather, it will give both sides a framework within which to relate to one another and ground rules declaring fair and unfair practices in that relationship. Using them, both sides can and, I believe, will soon learn what it takes to prevent a strike, something neither side wants. Strikes that do occur will be less frequent and less intense.

Such a law will not usher in the rule of sweet reason in labor-management relations. Indeed, there will probably be a brief initial period of heightened tension brought on by the stress of change. During this period, I expect, there will be a tendency among some public employers to use the new collective bargaining law as a scapegoat upon which to blame the discomfort that needed change often exerts on the old order. After this, however, things will settle down, and we will see the beginnings of intelligent compromise, civility, and more professional and sophisticated decision-making on both sides of the bargaining table.

Because the absence of federal collective bargaining legislation is not the sole cause of the troubles we confront in public sector labor-management relations, filling that void will not of itself solve those problems. Indeed, to the extent that the other root sources of those troubles are ignored, the effectiveness of a national collective bargaining law will be impaired. It is to the interest of the public, the public employer, and the public employee that these root problems be identified, their negative effects on public sector labor relations realized, and corrective action begun. Of the many such problems, three seem to demand priority attention.

One is inflation. With its dire consequences and subsequent dislocations likely to be spread wide among all members of our society, save for the very rich, it might seem a perversion to claim special distinction for public employers or employees as victims. But both groups do fall heirs to it.

Inflation already is hitting public employees hard because so many of them are still trying to catch up to private sector employees' wages. It is consigning them to life on an economic treadmill in which the gains made in the most recent contract settlement don't cover the increased costs of living in the preceding year.

Public employers, too, will be feeling the impact of inflation. We have, elsewhere in this book, considered the impact of voter resistance to swelling public budgets on the ability of elected officials to govern. The double-digit inflation that is rampant now should hit them with a force that will make their recent agonies seem a pleasure by comparison.

Another serious challenge to public sector labor relations is the future of government at the substate level. There exists not only the unconscionable dislocation of authority from responsibility on the municipal level about which I spoke in Chapter 5 but the accompanying evil of a zany mismatch between governmental powers and functions within the metropolitan area.

To the extent that the decrepit condition of local and municipal governance weakens the power of the chief executive to govern effectively — and they weaken it substantially in my experience — they weaken, too, his capacity to serve as a responsible partner at the bargaining table.

Rationality, responsiveness, and efficiency are called for, if local government is to meet the demands of present realities.

To be rational, a government must have, among other characteristics, a chief executive whose power is commensurate with his responsibilities — and those responsibilities must be defined broadly — and a clearly defined place within a larger system of governance, whose boundaries of geography and of power coincide with the boundaries of the metropolis, today's real city, or with the boundaries of even larger regions.

To be responsive a government needs a chief executive who can be systematically held accountable for the exercise of his powers and a radically altered form of decision-making, so that decisions are made at the level they can be made best — metropolitan, municipal, or neighborhood.

To be efficient, a government must have not only the capability to sort and spread out decisions to the levels at which they are made best; similarly, it must be able to sort out and assign service and enforcement functions to the levels at which they can be fulfilled best and most cheaply. There is little sense and a great deal of waste in permitting each of five townships within a metropolitan area to construct sewage treatment plants when one metropolitan or regional plant would treat the sewage better and at cheaper cost. Nor is there much sense or profit in dictating from on high to public service workers the solutions to problems with which they are more familiar than anyone.

Clearly, the changes required to meet the criteria of rationality, responsiveness, and efficiency run in two directions at once: toward greater power for the chief executive and simultaneously toward greater accountability from him for the use of his power; toward higher, metropolitan (or even regional) levels of governance and service delivery than are traditional in our system and toward lower, neighborhood levels of governance, even less in the traditional mold. The image of going two directions at once should not be permitted to obscure the fact that what would be involved in meeting these general criteria is a thoroughgoing reform of the lower end of the federal system of government aimed at both improving its problem-solving and service-providing capabilities and achieving greater enfranchisement of its citizens.

The third source of trouble for public sector labor relations is the fragmentation of the metropolitan economy, which has resulted in the declining economic health of many American cities. The geographical city of our traditions clearly has lost, or is losing, its preeminent place as an economic generator, the place where goods and services are made, sold, and exchanged; jobs created; wealth generated; and taxes collected. You don't need a degree in economics to know this is true. Your eyes can see the evidence of that decline in the decay into which the city has fallen.

For my part, I believe the economies of American cities will continue to sink into ill health for as long as we continue to define

cities by our present geography and ignore the clear evidence that the
real economic city is no longer just the "central," "inner," or "center"
city — take your choice of terms — but the entire metropolitan area.

Nevertheless the metropolitan area has not become the real city
in any social sense. Indeed, the generalization of the economy of
American cities to the metropolitan area has been accompanied by a
countertrend of social specialization. The suburbs, exurbs, and
satellite towns and cities that constitute the metropolitan area outside
of the old cities have become the places where, increasingly, the
middle class, largely white and youngish, lives. The old cities have
become the places where the very rich and the poor — poor blacks,
poor whites, and the poor old — are concentrated. Commerce, not
communication, characterizes the relationship between suburbs and
central cities.

In the majority of metropolitan areas the old city is denied its
rightful recognition as one of several economic generators within the
real city economy. Rather than being permitted to earn a share of the
product — the tax revenue — of that economy, through a
metropolitan taxing district, for example, it is restricted to its own tax
revenue to finance an increasingly heavy demand for services.

These, then, are three deeply rooted problems that directly affect
public sector employment and labor-management relations but are
not directly attacked by a Clay-Perkins bill.

There is a final *caveat* about what can be expected of such
legislation. It will not change the basic adversary nature of the
relationship between the public employer and employee over matters
of wages and working conditions. Nor should it. Imperfect as it is —
in labor relations as in law — the adversary system has the virtue of
making equity possible for both sides. We have found no alternative
that is better endowed.

What about the range of matters around which labor and
management should relate but to which the adversary system is not
productively applicable? Their existence, it seems to me, calls for the
creation of a second relationship, parallel to the adversary
relationship, which for want of a better term I will call a problem-
solving partnership. There is nothing in federally mandated collective
bargaining to discourage such a relationship; indeed, it is likely that
serious collective bargaining could commence building it.

As I envision it, such a partnership would operate internally
within the employer government to solve problems not soluble
through collective bargaining. The headlines are full of such a
problem in the field of education, which we can use as an illustrative

example: The censoring of school textbooks by community groups is causing both school boards and teachers very real problems, for the one political, for the other professional. Neither kind of problem can be solved by collective bargaining. But in a partnership, boards and teachers — employers and employees — could combine either to resist the onslaughts of parochialism, if that is the way they see their problem, as some have, or, for instance, to create a series of alternative schools that approach cultural pluralism in a different way, if that is their view of the challenge.

Such partnerships could also operate external to the employer government and community to deal with external problems. Inflation, the future of local government, and urban economic fragmentation are fit subjects around which to begin such a partnership. They have the added advantage of illustrating that these partnerships could operate on other than local governmental levels.

One of the several uncertainties inflation causes both public officials and public workers is the effect upon public services of the federal government's remedial economic actions. At the national level a partnership could, I believe, be formed between national employee organizations like those which are members of the Coalition of American Public Employees and national organizations of public officials like the League of Cities/Conference of Mayors. Such a partnership could monitor federal economic proposals to determine their likely effects on governance and public employment, speak out on such proposals, and lobby for their interests.

Similarly, the question of fragmentation of local governing authority could, imaginably, offer employer and employee groups within a state the opportunity for a problem-solving partnership aimed at getting a legislature to begin redesigning local governance.

And, a partnership erected on a metropolitan or regional base might, if it were ambitious, tackle the problem of restructuring a metropolitan economy. It is not beyond belief to consider that such a partnership might get help from others at both the local and national levels.

Although I advocate the creation of problem-solving partnerships like these and believe they can, and will, come into being, I am the first to acknowledge the obstacles that lie in their paths.

Chief among them is a set of attitudes that must begin to change if we are to take the first step toward partnership. For its part, management must be willing to awake from its dream of omnipotence, to shuck off the attitude that it has sole responsibility for solving all problems and, therefore, unlimited authority to concoct and impose all solutions. The reality of public life today is interdependence between power and performance, between the vested authority and his delegate, between boss and worker. Interdependence rules out the old hierarchical model of relationships and the command/response method of solving problems. In their places must be substituted a sharing of the problem-solving responsibility.

In modifying this attitude and preparing itself for a problem-solving relationship with labor, public management will find it futile to turn to private sector management for a model on which to pattern itself. Nowhere is the dream of management omnipotence dreamed more passionately than in conventional private management circles.

For its part, public sector labor must concede that labor organizations do, in fact, have a responsibility for the quality of the services their members provide, and they must act accordingly. In this, public sector labor cannot turn to the older, private sector labor unions for instruction.

Trade unions not only have failed to learn this lesson; they deny it and elevate their denial to the status of immutable wisdom. But, I wonder, how wise is it of the AFL-CIO to donate generously from union dues to the consumer movement, while denying vigorously their own institutional responsibility for solving one of the basic problems that movement was formed to deal with: shoddy, unsafe, unreliable goods produced by their own members?

Private sector labor is but a mirror image of private sector management. They share a distorted view not only of the consumer but of workers. They see their employees, their members, as solely economic beings whose chief satisfactions are economic, as entities to be served, controlled, and motivated economically.

There is a wider, more human, and truer view of American workers. Earlier in this book, I referred to studies published by Daniel Yankelovich that found that American attitudes toward work are changing for the better: more and more workers, but especially those under 35 and women, are seeking greater psychological rewards from their work. They want work, says Yankelovich, that is more meaningful, and they have an explicit definition of "meaningful": work in which they can become involved, committed, and interested; work that challenges them; and work that permits their participation in decision-making. Yankelovich also found that American workers are redefining success to give greater emphasis to personal self-fulfillment and less to traditional yardsticks like material possessions. But if the American work ethic is alive, it is not well, Yankelovich found, because the country's institutions — government, business, and labor unions — are not prepared to accommodate the growing insistence on meaningful work. Because these institutions do not provide meaningful work, those employees who expect it are experiencing a rising dissatisfaction with their jobs.

The drive toward work satisfaction began comparatively early among certain classes of public employees, especially teachers and social workers. I recall vividly the first strike ever to come to my attention that was called over noneconomic issues. It was in the mid-'60s. A group of social workers in California was striking for greater freedom from arbitrary rules that, in their professional judgment, prevented them from serving their clients according to the standards of their profession. Similarly, teachers in many parts of the country have come to place heavier and heavier emphasis in their negotiations on noneconomic matters that hinder them in doing a better job as professionals. Witness the list of strike issues set forth in Chapter 9.

There is no doubt that some of this emphasis stems from an understandable desire on the part of well-educated men and women (of recent years they often are better educated than many of their supervisors) to be treated with respect due their professional status rather than as very tall children, a tendency that is distressingly prevalent in many public service agencies. If professionalism breeds touchiness about professional status, it also breeds a concern on the part of the professional to achieve professional standards in his or her work. Anyone who cares to look will find this concern running as a deep current among public service professionals and, increasingly, among nonprofessionals who view their work in professional terms.

These are workers, then, who are concerned about the "quality" of their product, whether it is seen as counseling a dependent family, teaching history to a seventh grader, designing a new highway, or dealing with questions of law for the U.S. Treasury. What percentage of the public sector work force is committed to acting on this concern? That is an unknowable statistic. What is knowable, and more significant, is that their number is great enough to have placed these issues high on the agenda of public sector labor organizations.

In the years immediately ahead these concerns will assume greater importance among workers. And they will play their part in the union's internal affairs, guiding the selection of leaders who are as committed to acting on them as the growing body of members is.

What will such leaders find in the way of attitudes, concerns, and commitments on the other, the employer's, side of the table? The concern with the quality of public services seems, to me, to be less widespread among the ranks of management, than among the ranks of employees. At least, the willingness to use the labor-management forum as a place to hammer out action in this area appears to me to be stronger on the employee's than on his boss's side.

But that, too, is changing. One William Donaldson does not make a movement within the public management profession. But he is there in Tacoma after all, trying new ways of working with his employees to the end of better public service. And there are others like him in different parts of the country.

If the risks of a problem-solving partnership are high for such managers and labor leaders as may be willing to join them, so, too, are the possible rewards. Highest of all, in my judgment, is the chance to respond to workers' demands for more meaningful work within more human institutions, to bring about constructive and revolutionary changes in the ancient and fundamental relationship between workers and their jobs, and, in so doing, to provide a model for all managers and all labor leaders to follow.

How will we know when both sides have taken their first step toward new partnership? I know of no explicit criteria for judging. Nor do I think fast-moving events of this last quarter of the twentieth century will permit us to wait until, like a diamond cutter, we have found the precise place and moment to strike. Ours is a less tidy occupation than his; our final product is gained through a process that is cumulative rather than instant. To know when we are ready, we must first try.

Index

Academic freedom, 28
Administrative layers, 53
Administrators, 52, 53, 54
Adult education, 14
Adversary relationship, 102
Affluent people, 39
The Affluent Society, 19
Agency shop, 88
Albany, N.Y., 78
Amalgamated Transit Union, 2, 6
American Arbitration Association, 83, 85, 91
American Assembly, 34, 35, 51
American Federation of Labor, 9
AFL-CIO, 97, 104
American Railway Union, 6
Anderson, Arvid, 91, 92
Anderson, Wendell, 84
Arbitration, 86, 87, 89
Arden House, 34, 35, 46
Atlanta, Ga., 80
Auto industry, 7
Auto Lite workers, 8
Automation, 12
Autonomous school boards, 19
Average earnings, 23

Baltimore County, Md., 61, 73
Baltimore Evening Sun, 64
Baltimore, Md., 58, 60-73, 75, 76, 84
Baltimore Sun, 63
Bargaining rights, 79
Bernstein, Irving, 6, 8, 10
Best last offer, 87
Binding arbitration, 65, 87, 89
Blue Cross, 69
Blue Shield, 69

Boston, Mass., 22, 60
Budd Manufacturing Co., 7, 8, 93
Bundy, McGeorge, 48
Bureaucracy, 41
Bureaucratic featherbedding, 21
Bureau of Labor Statistics, 12, 16, 18
Business Week, 50

California, 105
California State Assembly, 15
California Teachers Association, 15
Canada, 89
Carnegie-Mellon University, 79, 91
Caseloads, 31, 51
Caseworkers, 51
Categories of employment, Bureau of Labor Statistics, 12
Centralization of powers, 77
Central Labor Council (Baltimore, Md.), 64
Charleston, S.C., 80
Checkoff of dues, 3
Cherry Hill, N.J., 80
Child abuse, 30
City council, 40, 57
Civil rights, 77, 78
Civil servants, 59
Civil Service List, 57
Civil Service systems, 19
Clay, William D. (Rep.), 88
Clay-Perkins Bill, 88-90, 94, 96, 97, 98, 99, 102
Coalition of American Public Employees, 73, 83-85, 90, 91, 96, 97, 98, 103
Collective bargaining, 1, 3, 4, 7-11, 20, 21, 34-36, 37, 39, 41-47, 49, 50, 58, 60, 68, 70, 71, 72, 76, 79, 80, 86, 91, 96, 98, 99, 100, 102, 103

"Collective Bargaining and the Munici-
  pal Employer," 35
"Collective Bargaining and the Union
  Leader," 35, 51
College administrators, 28
Commerce, 102
Communication, 102
Community college, 14
Company unions, 7, 8
Congress, 1, 11, 17, 85, 88, 91, 94, 97
Connors, Jack, 22
Conservative dogma, 77
"Constantine, John," 33, 51, 52-55, 98
Constitutional balance of powers, 77
Coolidge, Calvin, 58, 60
Corey, Arthur, 15
Costs of labor settlements, 38
Cost of Living Council, 79
Counterrepression, 82
Cramer, Ben, 63

Dallas Railway and Terminal Com-
  pany, 2
Dallas, Texas, 3, 5
Dallas Transit System, 2
Dead cats, 21, 35, 36, 38
Debs, Eugene, 6
Decade of the 1920s, 6
Decision-making, 52, 104
Demand for more pay, 36
Demand for services, 36
Degree of awareness, 73
Depression, 81
Des Moines Register, 26
Detroit, Mich., 48
Development Alternatives, Inc., 23
Development of precedents, 93
Dispute resolution, 95
Donaldson, William V., 48, 56, 57, 98,
  106
Dubuque, Iowa, 27

Economic force, 79
Economic incentives, 33
Economic power, 1
Economic quantification, 29
Economic status (of government work-
  ers), 23
Education, 13, 14, 103
Educational alternatives, 14, 15
Eley, Homer, 2, 4, 5
Employers (in 1930s), 8, 9, 10
Equity and the Public Employee
  (symposium), 83, 85, 91
Evaluation, 53, 54

Evans, Daniel, 84
Exclusive bargaining agent, 91
Executive branch, 85
Executive order, 7
Expansion of public services, 18

Fact-finding, 89
Fair practices, 99
Family Assistance Program, 17
Federal Civil Rights Act of 1964, 78
Federal demonstration grants, 4
Federal government, 1, 77, 78, 93
Federal government employment, 16,
  90
Federal intervention, 91
Federal involvement, 79
Federal legislation, 83, 84, 99
Federal Mediation and Conciliation
  Service, 89
Federal public employees labor rela-
  tions act, 84
Federal revenue sharing, 39, 61, 71
Federal-state approach, 93
Federal-state partnership, 91
Federal workers, 90
Finkelman, Jake, 90
Financial control, 50
Financial exigency, 27, 28
Firemen, 48, 57
Firefighters, 65, 71, 88
Firefighter's Union, 48, 56, 57, 97
Fiscal crisis, 39
Fiscal responsibility, 44
Ford, William (Rep.), 90
Ford Bill, 90
Fragmentation, 34, 40, 46, 59, 71, 101,
  103
Fraternal Order of Police, 70

Galbraith, John Kenneth, 19
Garbage, 48, 49, 59, 60, 64, 69, 72
Garbagemen, 60, 64, 65, 69
Garbage strike(s), 11, 73
Garbage workers, 75
General strike, 64, 76
Glover, R.L., 1-5
Good-faith bargaining, 87, 90, 91
Good government movement, 19
Goods-producing sector, 13
Gotbaum, Victor, 34, 35, 37, 38, 39, 41,
  42, 43, 45, 59, 60, 71
Government employers, 83
Government employee unions, 49
Government employment, 16
Government of the United States, 6

Governors, 39
Grievance procedure, 3, 4
Ground rules, 81, 82
Growth of public employment, 17
Guideline writers, 78

Haber, Herbert L., 55, 56
Hamilton, William R., and staff, 73
Harriman family, 34
Harriman, N.Y., 34
Hartman, Ambrose T., 62
Hawaii, 11
Haymarket Riot, 6
Herndon, Terry E., 85, 86, 94
High school teacher, 33, 51, 52-55
Highway workers, 62
Hillman, Robert S., 60, 62, 63, 65, 68
House Education and Labor Committee, 88
HR 8677, 88-90, 94, 96, 97, 98, 99, 102
Houston, Texas, 4
Huntsville, Ala., 80

Impasse, 89
Impasse resolution, 86, 87, 91, 93, 98
Independent commission, 40
Indochina War, 37
Industrial engineering, 50
Industries, 39
Industry, 50
Inflation, 35, 36, 37, 38, 46, 59, 73, 83, 95, 100, 103
In-hand wages, 25
Injunction, 62, 63, 65
Injunctive relief, 89
Illinois, 79
Insecurity of employment, 83
Interdependence, 104
International Association of Chiefs of Police, 72
International Association of Firefighters, 97
Involvement with work, 23, 104-105

Jail guards, 64, 75
Job security, 4, 25, 26
Johnson administration, 23, 24
Judicaid, 16
Judicare, 16

Kentucky, 7
King, Martin Luther, Jr., 69
Knights of Labor, 6

Labor and management, 82
Labor legislation, 97

Labor-management relations, 40, 43, 44, 45, 48, 58, 75, 80, 81, 83, 84, 91, 92, 99, 100, 102, 106
Labor Management Relations Service, 55, 56
The Labor Law Journal, 83
Labor peace, 81
Labor relations practitioners, 46
Labor strife, 18
Legal sanctions, 42
Lewis, Garfield, 7
Life adjustment, 17
"Life curriculum" 14, 15, 17
Lindsay, John, 49, 55, 56, 80
Little Rock, Ark., 80
Local 44, AFSCME, 60, 61, 62, 63, 67, 68, 69
Local 1195, AFSCME, 60, 62, 63, 66, 67, 68, 70
Local Division 1338, Amalgamated Transit Union, 2-5
Local governments, 49-50
Local power structures, 80
Longshoremen, 8
Los Angeles, Cal., 15
Loyalty, 37
Lumpert, Resi, 26, 27
Lumpert, Rolf, 26-27, 28

Macro images, 35
Maier, Henry W., 21, 34, 35, 36, 37, 38, 39, 40, 42, 43, 44, 45, 59, 60, 72
Management omnipotence, 104
Management rights, 50-51, 55
Mandel, Marvin, 66, 68, 70, 71, 72, 75
Mass walkouts, 11
Mayoral authority, 19
Mayors, 34, 35, 37, 39, 40, 42, 43, 44, 64, 75
McCarthy, Joseph (Sen.), 28
"The Meaning of Work," 23
Med-Arb technique, 86, 87
Mediation, 86, 89
Mediator, 89
Medicaid, 16, 55
Medicare, 16, 55
Memphis, Tenn., 11
Metropolitan areas, 13, 73-74, 102
Micro images, 35
Milwaukee, Wis., 21, 34, 35, 40, 43, 59
Minimum family income program, 17
Minneapolis, Minn., 8
Minnesota, 84
Minorities, 57
Monopolistic nature of public services, 42-43

Morss, Elliott, 23, 24
Multiple bargaining units, 86
Municipal economy, 47
Municipal labor agreement, 40
Municipal manpower, 36
Municipal taxing power, 19
Murphy, James W. (Judge), 62, 63, 64, 65, 68, 69, 70
Murray, Philip, 7

"Naked class conflict," 6, 10
National Association of Manufacturers, 8, 9
National Commission on Productivity, 49, 50
National Conference of Mayors, 103
National Education Association (NEA) 15, 20, 25, 79-80, 83, 85
National Governor's Conference, 40
National Industrial Recovery Act of 1933 (NIRA), 7, 8, 9
National Labor Board, 7, 8, 10
National Labor Relations Act (NLRA), 1, 85, 86, 88, 94, 95, 96, 97, 98
National Labor Relations Board (NLRB), 10, 88, 94, 95, 97, 98
National League of Cities, 40, 103
National Public Employees Relations Commission, 88, 90
National School Boards Association, 40
National Treasury Employees Union, 83
Necessary services, 59
Negotiations, 4, 42, 43, 44, 45, 68, 69, 87, 89
Negotiators, 44, 45, 60, 61, 69
New Deal, 8
"New grammar," 52
New Jersey, 80, 93
New York City, 34, 45, 49, 55
Newspapers, 9
Nixon administration, 17, 23, 24, 79
Nondelegable authority, 19

Occupational Safety and Health Act, 94
Office of Collective Bargaining, NYC, 91
Office of Economic Opportunity (OEO), 20
Ohio, 79, 93
Oregon, 84
Outcomes of inflation, 38

Paperwork, 32
Parent Teachers Association, 53
Parity understanding, 71
Parks, 16
Participatory decision making, 98
Participatory management, 56
Patrolmen, 56, 63, 67, 70
Pennsylvania, 11, 80
Pension benefits, 24, 25, 26
Pension costs, 44
Pension plan, 80
Periodic federal review, 91
Perkins, Carl D. (Rep.), 88
Points system, 62, 65, 68-69
Police, 63-74
Police chief, 56
Police job action, 63
Police strike, 58, 60, 66, 67, 69, 72, 73
Police union(s), 68, 71
Policy of the United States, 1
Political environments, 86
Political patronage, 79
Political power, 44
Politics, 59, 74
Pomerleau, Donald D., 63, 64, 66, 68, 70, 71, 72
Postindustrial society, 13
Pressman, Hyman, 65
Population projections, 28
Price inflation, 24
Private employees, 94
Private employment, 94
Private industry, 82
Private leaders, 76
"Private opulence and public squalor," 19
Private pension payments, 25
Private sector industry, 47
Private sector, 25, 28, 41, 42, 43, 45, 46, 47, 50, 81, 85, 86, 88, 91, 93, 94, 95, 96, 97, 98, 99, 100, 104
Private sector labor relations, 93
Private sector pension benefits, 25
Problems of metropolitan areas, 77
Problem-solving, 50, 101
Problem-solving partnership, 102-103, 104, 106
Product X factor, 17
Production of goods, 12
Productivity, 47, 49, 50, 55, 98
Productivity bargaining, 50, 98
Professional status, 105
Professorial tenure, 26-28
Property tax, 38, 39, 61
Provision of services, 59

Public employee earnings, 23, 24
Public employees, 11, 22, 23, 24, 25, 26,
    29, 33, 34, 36, 38, 39, 41, 43, 46, 47,
    56, 76, 78, 79, 82, 83, 84, 91, 92, 93,
    94, 95, 96, 100, 102
Public Employees Relations Board, 91
Public employees rights, 74
Public employee unionism, 79
Public employers, 21, 25, 26, 34, 39, 41,
    43, 46, 76, 78, 99, 100, 102
Public employment, 18, 19, 26, 29, 36,
    79, 82, 94, 103
Public labor, 10, 28
Public labor relations, 34, 46, 71, 95
Public management, 10, 79, 104, 106
Public managers, 59, 106
Public officials, 50, 55
Public opinion, 73-75
Public pension systems, 24
Public relations, 45
Public school teachers, 11
Public sector, 10, 16, 18, 19, 21, 28, 39,
    41, 42, 43, 45, 46, 47, 50, 58, 59, 75,
    76, 77, 79, 80, 81, 82-89, 91, 92, 93, 94,
    95, 96, 97, 98, 99, 100, 104, 105
Public sector collective bargaining, 21
Public sector labor relations, 18, 19, 39,
    47, 59, 77, 79, 84, 87, 89, 91, 92, 93,
    95, 100, 101
"Public servant(s)," 20, 36
Public services, 13
Public Service Staff Relations Act
    (Canada), 90
Public Service Staff Relations Board
    (Canada), 90
Public service unions, 38
Public service workers, 101
Public workers, 10, 19, 36, 59
Public Workers and Public Unions, 35,
    51
Pullman Company, 6

Quality, 47, 59, 105
Quantification, 47

Rapanotti, Thomas, 68, 70
Rate of taxation, 39, 61, 71
Recognition, 23, 28, 29, 83
Reece, Florence, 9
Reform instinct, 19
Reliability, 59
Reprisals, 69, 70, 75, 90
Retirement benefits, 25, 37
Retirement systems, 25, 95
Reuther, Walter, 37
Revenge, 80

Rhetoric, 50, 55, 92, 93
Right to bargain, 79
Right to organize, 6, 7, 77
Right to protect labor, 10
Right to strike, 11, 58, 74, 75, 76, 89
Rising expectations, 83
Rockefeller, Nelson, 80
Roosevelt, Franklin, 7, 8, 9
Rosow, Jerome, 23
Rydor, Thomas, 26, 27

Sacramento, Cal., 78
Sanctioned strike, 62
San Francisco, Cal., 11, 76
Sanitation workers, 48, 49, 62, 63, 64
Schaefer, William Donald, 61, 62, 63,
    67, 71, 72, 75
School boards, 53, 80
Scottsdale, Ariz., 56
Section 7(a) National Industrial Rec-
    overy Act, 7, 9, 10
Security, 4, 19
Self-fulfillment, 104
Senate (U.S.), 9
Separate coverage, 85, 87
Service-producing element, 16
Service-producing industries, 12-13
Severance pay, 80
Shaw, George Bernard, 19
Shriver, Sargent, 20
Social attitudes, 18-19, 21, 77
Social compact, 28
Social learning, 82, 84
Social Security Act, 92
Social services, 51
Social workers, 17, 29, 30, 31, 32, 33,
    88, 105
State and federal financial aid, 38
State and local retirement benefits, 25
State Board of Certification (Cal.), 15
State-federal approach, 92
State governments, 16, 77, 78, 79, 93
State laws, 10, 79, 80
State legislature (Md.), 61
State level, 77, 78
Stetson, Damon, 55
Stewart, John M., 49, 50
Stokes, Carl B., 58, 76
Strike(s), 7, 8, 11, 18, 21, 42, 59, 60-73,
    79, 80, 82, 89, 96, 99, 105
Students, 52, 54, 55
Supervisors, 95, 105
Supply of teachers, 15
Supreme Court (U.S.), 9
Sympathy, 73-79

Tacoma Fire Fighters Union, 57
Tacoma, Wash., 48, 49, 56, 57, 106
Tallahassee, Fla., 78
Tamm, Quinn, 72
Tax dollars, 47, 59
Taxpayers, 38
Tax rate in Maryland, 61
Tax revenues, 71, 102
Teachers, 51, 52, 53, 54, 60, 64, 71, 80,
    103, 105
*Teacher Supply and Demand in Public
    Schools,* 15
Teaching, 33, 51-55
Tenure, 26-28
Tenure acts, 95
Testimonial dinner, 22
Texas, 1, 2, 10
Texas Civil Statutes, 3
Time constraints, 89
Toledo, Ohio, 8
Trade employment, 16
Trade unions, 104
Tradition, 51
Traditional organizing pattern, 85
Traditional service categories, 13
Traditional services, 16
Transit strikes, 11
Truckers, 8
The Turbulent Years, 6

Unfair labor practices, 90, 91, 93, 99
Union involvement in politics, 74
Union leader(s), 37, 38, 41, 42, 43, 45,
    48, 49, 50, 56, 62, 76, 97, 105-106
Union membership, 95
Union organizing drives, 7
Union(s), 1, 3-10, 36, 37, 38, 39, 40, 41,
    42, 43, 44, 45, 48, 49, 50, 55, 56, 62,
    74, 76, 80, 88, 91, 95, 97, 105, 106
The Unions and the Cities, 25
Union security, 80
Union shop, 88
United Auto Workers, 37
United Mine Workers, 6, 7
United States, 55
U.S. Conference of Mayors, 40

U.S. labor force, 16
U.S. Treasury, 105
University of Dubuque, 26, 27
University of Iowa, 26
Urban apocalypse, 35
Urban renewal programs, 78

Veillette, Peter, 25

Wages and salaries, 25
Wagner Act, 1, 6, 10, 11, 81 - 85, 90, 98,
    99
Wagner, Robert F. Sr. (Sen.), 8, 9
Washington, D.C., 23, 39, 73, 78
Washington Post, 61, 67
Wayne, John, 51
Weber, Arnold, 79, 80, 91, 92
Weirton Steel Co., 7, 8, 93
Welfare structure, 51
Weisenfeld, Allan, 83
Wellington, Harry H., 25
West Coast, 8
West Germany, 27
"We Will Overcome," 9
"Which Side Are You On," 9
White House, 7
Wildcat strike, 62
"Williams, Marian," 29-33
Winter, Ralph K., Jr., 25
Wise, Helen, 79-80
Workmen's compensation, 93
*The Worker and the Job: Coping with
    Change,* 23
Worker productivity, 47-49
Work ethic, 23, 104
Work week, 48
World War II, 13, 79
Wurf, Jerry, 63, 66, 83

Yankelovich, Daniel, 23, 104-105
Year 1933, 7
Year 1934, 6, 7, 10, 81
Yearly rate of inflation, 73
Young, Coleman, 84

Zagoria, Sam, 35, 51